Living in Ancient Rome

EXPLORING CULTURAL HISTORY

Don Nardo, *Book Editor*

Daniel Leone, *President*
Bonnie Szumski, *Publisher*
Scott Barbour, *Managing Editor*

GREENHAVEN
PRESS®

THOMSON
———＊———™
GALE

San Diego • Detroit • New York • San Francisco • Cleveland
New Haven, Conn. • Waterville, Maine • London • Munich

LIBRARY OF CONGRESS CATALOGING-IN-PUBLICATION DATA

Living in ancient Rome / Don Nardo, book editor.
    p. cm. — (Exploring cultural history)
  Includes bibliographical references and index.
  ISBN 0-7377-1456-5 (lib. : alk. paper) — ISBN 0-7377-1457-3 (pbk. : alk. paper)
  1. Rome—Social life and customs. I. Nardo, Don, 1947– . II. Series.
DG78.L6 2004
937—dc21
                                                                        2002040816

Printed in the United States of America

Contents

Chapter 2: In Society: Religion, Weddings, and Roads

Chapter 3: Leisure Time: Large and Small-Scale Games

Foreword

Too often, history books and teachers place an overemphasis on events and dates. Students learn that key births, battles, revolutions, coronations, and assassinations occurred in certain years. But when many centuries separate these happenings from the modern world, they can seem distant, disconnected, even irrelevant.

The reality is that today's society is *not* disconnected from the societies that preceded it. In fact, modern culture is a sort of melting pot of various aspects of life in past cultures. Over the course of centuries and millennia, one culture passed on some of its traditions, in the form of customs, habits, ideas, and beliefs, to another, which modified and built on them to fit its own needs. That culture then passed on its own version of the traditions to later cultures, including today's. Pieces of everyday life in past cultures survive in our own lives, therefore. And it is often these morsels of tradition, these survivals of tried and true past experience, that people most cherish, take comfort in, and look to for guidance. As the great English scholar and archaeologist Sir Leonard Woolley put it, "We cannot divorce ourselves from our past. We are always conscious of precedents . . . and we let experience shape our views and actions."

Thus, for example, Americans and the inhabitants of a number of other modern nations can pride themselves on living by the rule of law, educating their children in formal schools, expressing themselves in literature and art, and following the moral precepts of various religions and philosophies. Yet modern society did not invent the laws, schools, literature, art, religions, and philosophies that pervade it; rather, it inherited these things from previous cultures. "Time, the great destroyer, is also the great preserver," the late, noted thinker Herbert J. Muller once observed. "It has preserved . . . the immense accumulation of products, skills, styles, customs, institutions, and ideas that make the man on the American street indebted to all the peoples of history, including some who never saw a street." In this way, ancient Mesopotamia gave the world its first cities and literature; ancient Egypt, large-scale architecture; ancient Israel, the formative concepts of Judaism,

Christianity, and Islam; ancient Greece, democracy, the theater, Olympic sports, and magnificent ceramics; ancient China, gunpowder and exotic fabrics; ancient Rome and medieval England, their pioneering legal systems; Renaissance Italy, great painting and sculpture; Elizabethan England, the birth of modern drama; and colonial America, the formative environments of the founders of the United States, the most powerful and prosperous nation in world history. Only by looking back on those peoples and how they lived can modern society understand its roots.

Not all the products of cultural history have been so constructive, however. Most ancient Greeks severely restricted the civil rights and daily lives of women, for instance; the Romans kept and abused large numbers of slaves, as did many Americans in the years preceding the Civil War; and Nazi Germany and the Soviet Union curbed or suppressed freedom of speech, assembly, and religion. Examining these negative aspects of life in various past cultures helps to expose the origins of many of the social problems that exist today; it also reminds us of the ever-present potential for people to make mistakes and pursue misguided or destructive social and economic policies.

The books in the Greenhaven Press Exploring Cultural History series provide readers with the major highlights of life in human cultures from ancient times to the present. The family, home life, food and drink, women's duties and rights, childhood and education, arts and leisure, literacy and literature, roads and means of communications, slavery, religious beliefs, and more are examined in essays grouped by theme. The essays in each volume have been chosen for their readability and edited to manageable lengths. Many are primary sources. These original voices from a past culture echo through the corridors of time and give the volume a strong feeling of immediacy and authenticity. The other essays are by historians and other modern scholars who specialize in the culture in question. An annotated table of contents, chronology, and extensive bibliography broken down by theme add clarity and context. Thus, each volume in the Greenhaven Press Exploring Cultural History series opens a unique window through which readers can gaze into a distant time and place and eavesdrop on life in a long vanished culture.

Introduction: Roman Life—
The Struggle for Survival
and Upward Mobility

Everyday life for nearly all ancient Romans consisted of a struggle of one kind or another. For some, the main struggle was to earn a living and make ends meet. The poorest in society, for example, worked from dawn to dusk, day after day, year after year, the farmer trying to keep from starving, and the slave striving to please the master and avoid a beating. Those in somewhat better situations, including shopkeepers, factory workers, craftsmen, soldiers, and entertainers, usually had enough to eat but still faced long years of hard work for minimal pay.

In contrast, the wealthy and powerful, who made up only a small fraction of the population, did not have to worry about making a living. The primary struggle for them was often achieving upward mobility—improvements in one's social status, prestige, influence, and so forth. At least in their case few obstacles barred their way to moving up in life. Members of the privileged classes shared a feeling of superiority over people of lesser means; also, the wealthy and powerful made the laws, set social standards, and usually readily accepted and helped others of privilege in a system often referred to today as an "old boys club."

Members of the lower and underprivileged classes frequently struggled to achieve upward mobility, too. But it was much more difficult for them to achieve significant gains in social status. Centuries of tradition, bolstered by numerous laws and social restrictions created by the wealthy, influential men of Rome's old boys club, had cemented into place a rather rigid social ladder. Those occupying its upper rungs jealously guarded their privileged positions. This made it hard for those on the lower rungs, including women as well as slaves and poorer folk, to make significant gains in social status, respect, and self-esteem.

Thus, the struggle for upward mobility, accompanied by the daily fight for basic survival among the lower classes, was an integral feature of Roman society, one that affected people of all social classes and rank. And not surprisingly, there evolved strict traditions and rules emphasizing the differences in social rank and the privileges or lack thereof associated with each rank. This highly ingrained and usually very rigid social system was called patronage.

The Root of Roman Society

In the original Roman patronage system, the heads of well-to-do families became the patrons (*patroni*) of less well-off clients (*clientes*). A patron's dependent clients usually voted as he directed, did him all sorts of favors, and supported him in other ways in exchange for his financial and legal protection. In addition, freed slaves were expected to become the clients of their former masters. "The very root of Roman society," noted scholar Michael Grant comments, "was the institution of a relatively few rich patrons . . . linked with their more numerous poor clients."[1]

One way that poorer clients were expected to show respect and subservience to their patrons was through the *salutatio*, or "morning salute." It consisted of a group of clients paying a morning visit to their patron's home. There he would greet them, perhaps assign them tasks to fulfill the favors they owed him, if they were lucky give them gifts or invite them to dinner, and/or simply give them a nod and go about his business. Sometimes a patron would not even bother with a nod. In a passage from one of his surviving essays, the Roman playwright Seneca the Younger describes the rude behavior of a number of snooty upper-class patrons:

> How many patrons are there who drive away their clients by staying in bed when they call, or ignoring their presence, or being rude? How many are there who rush off on a pretense of urgent business after keeping the poor client waiting for a long time? . . . How many, still hung-over and half-asleep from the last night's drinking, will yawn disdainfully at men who have interrupted their own sleep in order to wait upon his awakening?[2]

Patronage did not always involve such clear-cut differences between rich and poor and privileged and underprivileged, however. The system eventually extended throughout the ranks of Roman society. Though a well-to-do aristocrat had many clients of his own, he, in turn, was client to someone even more wealthy or powerful. The only limit set on this ascending ladder of social importance was the position of emperor during the centuries of the Roman Empire. Members of Rome's highest elite—military generals, senators, millionaires, and so forth—actively sought and benefited from the emperor's patronage.

The patronage system, which affected the lives and fortunes of people of all walks of life and controlled the corridors of upward mobility, was so ingrained that parts of it survived Rome's fall. As classical scholar Jo-Ann Shelton observes:

> The patronage system was one of the most deep-rooted and pervasive aspects of ancient Roman society. It has endured into modern Italian society where a *pardone,* or "godfather," offers protection and assistance to those less wealthy and powerful than himself, and in turn acquires a "clientele" of loyal supporters.[3]

Obstacles in the Road to Social Improvement

Many ancient and modern authors have provided detailed descriptions of the struggle for upward mobility of Roman men, particularly the rich and famous. Often given little space or neglected entirely in the history books are similar struggles by members of the lower and underprivileged classes. The two largest and most important of these groups were freedmen (freed slaves, both male and female) and women. Their strivings for survival, recognition, and when possible better lives were noteworthy, difficult, and sometimes painful.

As for freedmen, their struggle to survive in Roman society was somewhat different than that of slaves, from whose ranks they had come. Slaves' lives were difficult and often unrewarding, to be sure. However, many slaves were able to carve out reasonably safe and comfortable niches for themselves in households, especially those of the well-to-do. Like other slaves, they lacked the ability to control their own destinies and sometimes endured physical abuse. But on the positive side, they did not have to worry about paying the rent and putting food on the table.

By contrast, freedmen did face the necessity of making a living. Because they enjoyed some freedom of upward mobility in society, they often attempted to better themselves by finding more lucrative jobs or meeting and exploiting relationships with wealthy or influential Romans. Yet society placed many restrictions on ambitious freedmen. The fact was that most freeborn Romans refused to accept former slaves as complete equals, no matter how talented, loyal, or honest they might be. The stigma of having once been a slave simply could not be erased in a society in which slaves remained a despised class.

Freedmen might escape the shackles of that class in one of several ways. Many bought their freedom using their savings (the *peculium*) consisting of a small but regular allowance many masters gave well-behaved slaves. Evidence suggests that some slaves were so eager to increase their savings for this purpose that they periodically starved themselves so that they could sell portions of their food rations for a profit. The price a slave had to pay for freedom varied widely. Some masters no doubt demanded enough money to help defray the costs of years of feeding and clothing the slave. Other masters freed female slaves as a reward for having a certain number of children (who were automatically the slaves of those masters). One such master, wealthy estate owner L. Junius Columella, wrote:

> To women . . . who are unusually prolific, and who ought to be rewarded for the bearing of a certain number of offspring, I have granted exemption from work and sometimes even freedom. . . . To a mother of three sons exemption from work was granted; to a mother of more her freedom as well.[4]

Similarly, some slaves became freedmen when kind masters gave them freedom to reward their years of loyalty and good service. Mutual affection and even genuine feelings of brotherly or fatherly love might also be involved, as in the case of the famous orator Cicero and his freedman, Tiro. When the former slave became ill, Cicero wrote to him: "For myself, I long for your presence, but it is as one who loves you; love urges 'Let me see you in good health'; longing [urges] 'let it be with all speed.'"[5]

Still other freedmen escaped slavery thanks to their intellectual and literary talents. (Many were Greeks or other foreigners who had been well schooled before being captured and enslaved.) The Roman historian Suetonius mentions several examples, including that of Lucius Plotus, who as a slave had been chained near his master's front door. "He was set free because of his talent and interest in letters," said Suetonius.

Then becoming a teacher of rhetoric [persuasive public speaking],
he had [the illustrious military leader] Pompey the Great for a
pupil, and wrote a history of [Pompey's] exploits. . . . He was the
first of all freedmen to take up the writing of history, which up to
that time had been confined to men of the highest position.[6]

Plotus was more fortunate than most other freedmen, who
had to choose from less creative and prestigious professions. The
majority of freeborn Romans, particularly those with moderate
or considerable means, viewed most kinds of menial, financial,
and administrative positions as degrading or unsuitable. And
freedmen (often aided by slaves of their own) were expected to
take such jobs. Therefore, the careers open to freedmen had limited prestige and importance in the eyes of the upper classes and
society in general.

Still, these occupations could be quite varied in their nature
and the degree of skill needed to perform them. The more educated freedmen included managers in the trades and industries,
financial dealers, teachers, scribes, secretaries, and doctors. Freedmen having less education and fewer skills worked alongside
slaves and lower-class freeborn Romans in less prestigious professions. Males were often laborers, as well as foremen, for example, on construction sites; both males and females worked as
entertainers such as gladiators, actors, singers, dancers, and musicians; and probably a majority of prostitutes were freedwomen.
In addition, freedwomen often performed as weavers, spinners,
wool workers, and mill and bakery workers, although a few held
more responsible or influential positions, such as landlady,
moneylender, or shopkeeper.

Women's Struggle for Emancipation

The fact that most working women were restricted to such
unglamorous professions is revealing. Like freedmen, women in
Rome faced a constant uphill battle for recognition, respect, and
personal autonomy in a society tightly controlled by a small
group of well-to-do, powerful men. This was plainly unfair considering that many women played essential roles that society simply could not do without. First, Roman women of all classes gave
birth to and raised sons to run the state and fight the wars. Some
upper-class women advised powerful sons or husbands behind

the scenes; maintained the flame burning in the state hearth; and had important duties in state religious festivals. Meanwhile, women across the Roman realm organized and ran households, shopped and traded in marketplaces, and worked as laborers.

Despite these efforts, most Roman women remained second-class citizens. Like women in other ancient societies, they were subject to the authority of their husbands, fathers, sons, and other male figures and did not enjoy the same rights and social prominence as male citizens. An exception was in the area of religion. Although women in Rome could not vote or hold public office at any time in Rome's long history, they *could* become public priestesses, who were highly respected. (Only a tiny minority of women were ever chosen for this task, however.)

In general, male treatment of women as inferiors stemmed from men's belief that they were more intelligent and competent than women. According to Cicero: "Our ancestors established the rule that all women, because of their weakness of intellect, should be under the power of guardians."[7] These guardians were always men, who controlled the property of women and barred them from initiating divorce, making wills, and other legal procedures.

Fortunately for women, by the first century B.C. society had become somewhat less chauvinistic in its treatment of women. Cicero's writings and those of other men of his day reveal a certain relaxation of traditional, strict male control of women. It would be an exaggeration to call it emancipation in the modern sense of the word; and examples of upward mobility among women in society remained few. But the lot of at least some women had improved measurably since early Roman times, a trend that would continue. Though they never managed to gain any political rights, many women were allowed to file for divorce at will and to inherit and control their own property. Also, a few came to administer quite sizable fortunes.

Upper-Class Women

In fact, the privileges and benefits of being born into families with wealth and high social rank allowed a tiny handful of women to wield some real, though usually indirect, political power. Some wives, mothers, and daughters of army officers and politicians, and even emperors, groomed their sons for high office. Others pestered, begged, offered advice to, or otherwise influenced their husbands behind the scenes. And still others took part in dangerous schemes and conspiracies to advance their own or their families' interests. These are the Roman women the modern world knows most about, since most of the surviving written evidence describes them, rather than poorer women.

One crucial factor that helped improve the personal autonomy and chances for upward mobility of upper-class women was their education. They were better educated than lower-class women (as well as many lower-class men). And reading and writing skills increased their chances of success in managing money, estates, business affairs, and political intrigues. Educational opportunities for upper-class young women were well established by the third century B.C. Their families sent them to a private elementary school, where an instructor (usually a freedman) taught them basic reading and writing skills and some simple arithmetic. At about the age of eleven, girls usually left school. Some continued their education at home, receiving instruction from their parents or paid tutors.

Some of the fathers who educated their daughters in this manner did so because they thought it would better their chances of attracting suitable high-placed husbands. However, at least a few fathers came to believe that educating women was also the fair and ethical thing to do. "Women have received from the gods the same ability to reason that men have," noted the first-century A.D. philosopher and teacher Musonius Rufus in a rationale for educating women.

> Women have the same senses as men, sight, hearing, smell, and all the rest. . . . In addition, it is not men alone who possess eagerness and a natural inclination towards virtue, but women also. Women are pleased no less than men by noble and just deeds, and reject the opposite of such actions. . . . It is reasonable, then, for me to think that women ought to be educated similarly to men in respect of virtue, and they must be taught starting when they are children.[8]

Those Roman men who shared Musonius's progressive views about women were apparently in the minority. Men continued to dominate, marginalize, and stereotype women; and the traditional Roman matron—the dutiful, obedient wife and mother—

still symbolized old-fashioned Roman virtues. Furthermore, most male writers automatically viewed and measured the women of their own day in these terms. For example in the 40s A.D., while in exile (after being accused of having an affair with an emperor's sister), Seneca the Younger wrote a long letter to cheer up his despondent mother. He praised her for maintaining her old-fashioned Roman values, such as austerity and modesty, saying:

> Unchastity, the greatest plague of our age, has put the majority of womankind in a different category from yours; gems nor pearls have tempted you; its glitter has not persuaded you that wealth is man's greatest good. You were well brought up in an old-fashioned and strict household, and you have never been led astray by the imitation of worse women, which is a hazard even to good ones. You have never been ashamed of your children, as though their number taunted you with your years. . . . You have not defiled your face with paint and . . . cosmetics; you never fancied sheer dresses that revealed as much on as off. Your unique jewel, your fairest beauty, which time cannot wither, your greatest glory, is your proven modesty.[9]

Working Women

Needless to say, the vast majority of Roman women were not so fortunate as to hail from a well-to-do family, as Seneca's mother did, and had limited chances for upward mobility in society. Many lower-class women dutifully kept house for their husbands and children. But large numbers had to work. And as in the case of freed slaves, their inferior social status dictated the kinds of jobs they could take. In fact, a large proportion of working women *were* freedwomen (as well as slaves). For example, freedwomen and female slaves did all the spinning and most of the weaving in the many cloth-making shops that existed in Rome and other towns.

In addition, freedwomen (as well as some freeborn lower-class women) acted as midwives, wet nurses, clothes makers, actresses, singers, dancers, musicians, mill and bakery workers, fishmongers, letter carriers, and farm workers, among other jobs. Most prostitutes were probably freedwomen as well (others being slaves and freeborn women).

A few lower-class women even ventured into roles and occupations usually filled only by men. There is evidence for cases of female doctors, writers, and business owners, for instance. The first-century A.D. Roman naturalist and encyclopedist Pliny the Elder reported:

> Women, too, have been painters. Iaia of Cyzzieus, who never married, worked in Rome during the youth of Marcus Varro [in the late second and early first centuries B.C.]. She used both the painter's brush and, on ivory, the graving tool. She painted women most frequently, including a panel picture of an old woman in Naples, and even a self-portrait for which she used a mirror. No one's hand was quicker to paint a picture than hers; so great was her talent that her prices far exceeded those of the most celebrated painters of her day . . . whose works fill the [art] galleries.[10]

Cases of women gladiators have also been documented. Society viewed male gladiators as disreputable characters and expected women to know their place, so the gladiatrix was generally seen as especially uncouth. It is true that women who fought in the arena were far less numerous than the men who did so. But they did come briefly into style from time to time. Common "stage" names for female gladiators were Achillia (a feminine form of Achilles, the warrior-hero of the Greek epic poem the *Iliad*), and Amazon (a reference to the legendary race of warrior women in Greek mythology). The second-century A.D. satirist Juvenal, who made fun of numerous aspects of society, had particular venom for the gladiatrix:

> And what about . . . our lady sword-fighters. We've all seen *them,* stabbing the stump with a sword, shield well advanced, going through the proper motions. . . . The goal of all their practice is the real arena. But then, what modesty can be looked for in some helmeted vixen, a renegade from her sex, who thrives on masculine violence? . . . What a fine sight for some husband—*it might be you*— his wife's equipment put up at auction! . . . [Or] imagine your delight when the dear girl sells off her greaves [lower leg protectors]! . . . Note how she snorts at each practice thrust, bowed down by the weight of her helmet . . . then wait for the laugh, when she lays down her weapons and squats over the potty![11]

The Struggle for Water

Working women struggled not only in their jobs, but also to maintain safe and comfortable, if small and simply furnished, households, whether in the cities or rural villages and farms.

Whether they were freeborn, freedmen, or slaves, most members of the lower and working classes who lived in Rome and other urban areas dwelled in small rented apartments. Many such units made up a multistoried tenement block called an *insula* ("island"). As pointed out by Juvenal, who lived in one, these structures were usually poorly built, rundown, and dangerous. "We live in a city," he wrote,

> which is, to a great extent, propped up by flimsy boards. The manager of your apartment building stands in front of the collapsing structure and, while he conceals a gaping crack . . . he tells you to "sleep well"—even though a total cave-in is imminent! It's best, of course, to live where there are no fires and no panics in the dead of night. Here, one neighbor discovers a fire and shouts for water, [while] another neighbor moves out his shabby possessions.[12]

In contrast, Rome's small minority of wealthy families lived in much larger, more luxurious, and safer individual townhouses. There was a great gap, therefore, between the everyday comforts of the well-to-do, who did not have to struggle to make ends meet and enjoyed real chances for upward mobility, and those of the vast majority who found it difficult to escape the squalor of the tenements. This gap is well illustrated by a single reality of life for all in Rome—the need for fresh water. The water supply for the Roman capital came mainly from aqueducts, long stone channels that carried the precious liquid to the city from mountain streams and lakes many miles away. By A.D. 206, Rome was served by eleven aqueducts that brought in a total of perhaps 250 million gallons a day.

Emperors, senators, military leaders, and other highly placed individuals were allowed to run private water lines to the main incoming channels. These lines ended in sinks equipped with bronze faucets not much different than those in modern kitchens and bathrooms. Owners of large businesses and a few others were also sometimes granted special permission to receive aqueduct water privately. According to Sextus Julius Frontinus, who served as Rome's water commissioner in the late first-century A.D., "No one shall draw water from the public supply without a license. . . . Whoever wishes to draw water for private use must seek for a grant and bring to the commissioner a writing [official permit] from the emperor."[13]

The tenants of the *insulae* were not so fortunate. They had to get the daily supplies of water they required for drinking and cooking from public fountains, which received water from the aqueducts via underground pipes. The vast majority of city-dwellers walked to the nearest fountain, filled up their buckets, and trudged home. To make this chore as painless as possible, the water commission usually tried to place public fountains no more than 260 feet apart. This way, most Romans had access to clean aqueduct water within a radius of about 130 feet of their homes.

Still, carrying heavy buckets of water up two, three, or more stories one to three times a day was a chore that many people sought to avoid if they could. So, though the law forbade private use of the water from the aqueducts except by a privileged few, many people ignored the law and proceeded to divert water secretly from these channels. Sometimes they bribed maintenance workers and other members of the water commission to help them tap into the aqueducts. This problem of water theft was often serious and widespread, as Frontinus discovered when he carefully inspected the aqueducts shortly after becoming water commissioner. In his initial report, he noted widespread cheating, particularly by people living near the aqueducts. "The cause of this," he said,

> is the dishonesty of the water-men [hired by former water commissioners], whom we have detected diverting water from the public conduits for private use. But a large number of landowners also, past whose fields the aqueducts run, tap the conduits. . . . We have found irrigated fields, shops, garrets [houses of prostitution] even, and lastly . . . [private] houses fitted up with fixtures through which a constant supply of flowing water might be assured.[14]

Frontinus also provided some specific examples of how the water commission workers defrauded the system, including a method known as "puncturing":

> There are extensive areas in various places where secret pipes run under the pavements all over the city. I discovered that these pipes are furnishing water by special branches to all those engaged in business in those localities through which the pipes ran, being drilled for that purpose here and there by the so-called "puncturers". . . . How large an amount of water has been stolen in this manner, I estimate by means of the fact that a considerable quan-

tity of lead has been brought in by the removal [at Frontinus's order] of that kind of [illegal] branch pipes.[15]

Frontinus made sure that the water thieves were prosecuted. The law demanded that violators pay a stiff fine, plus repair any damage they had done to the aqueducts. (In the case of a slave stealing water, the master was required to pay the fine.)

Threats to Peace and Safety

Other aspects of living in Rome made it difficult for lower-class persons with limited chances of moving up in life to enjoy a peaceful, safe existence. Some people dumped garbage and even sewage out their windows and there was a constant danger of falling roofing tiles and flower pots. "You'll be thought . . . [a] fool," Juvenal quipped, "if you don't make your will before venturing out to dinner."[16]

Also, walking the streets after dark could be dangerous. Juvenal himself was attacked one night, bitterly writing later: "This is the poor man's freedom: having been mugged and battered with fists, he begs . . . his assailant to allow him to go away with a few teeth left."[17] Juvenal also complained about the threat of burglars robbing apartments.

Added to these problems was the city's incessant noise. According to the humorist Martial, a younger contemporary of Juvenal's:

> There is no place in the city where a poor man may have a quiet moment for thought. . . . Before dawn bakers disturb you; and the whole day the hammers of coppersmiths jar your nerves. Over here the moneychanger idly jangles . . . coins on his filthy table. Over there . . . the frenzied band of [the war goddess] Bellona's priests never stops chanting; nor does the sailor, who survived a shipwreck but lost a limb, ever cease his begging.[18]

Martial was quick to point out the stark contrast between the chaos endured by the common people and the relative calm enjoyed by the wealthy set in their townhouses in nicer areas of the city. "You, Sparsus, know nothing of these things," the humorist wrote,

> you who enjoy the luxury of a mansion, you whose home looks down on the hilltops, you who own a country estate right here

in Rome. . . . You enjoy a deep sleep and a stillness disturbed by
no voices.[19]

Such were some of the differences between the struggles of the
underpaid, underprivileged, and underappreciated and those fortunate few who enjoyed an easier climb up Rome's often unfor-
giving social ladder.

Notes

1. Michael Grant, *A Social History of Greece and Rome.* New York: Charles Scribner's Sons, 1992, p. 50.

2. Seneca, *An Essay About the Brevity of Life,* excerpted in Jo-Ann Shelton, ed.
   and trans., *As the Romans Did: A Source Book in Roman Social History.* New
   York: Oxford University Press, 1988, p. 17.

3. Shelton, *As the Romans Did,* p. 14.

4. Columella, *On Agriculture,* trans. H.B. Ash et al. 3 vols. Cambridge, MA:
   Harvard University Press, 1960, vol. 1, p. 95.

5. Cicero, *Letters to His Friends,* trans. W. Glynn Williams. 3 vols. Cambridge,
   MA: Harvard University Press, 1965, vol. 3, p. 319.

6. Suetonius, *On Rhetoricians,* trans. J.C. Rolfe, in *Works.* 2 vols. Cambridge,
   MA: Harvard University Press, 1965, vol. 2, p. 443.

7. Cicero, *For Murena,* in *Cicero: On Government,* trans. Michael Grant. New
   York: Penguin Books, 1993, p. 123.

8. Quoted in Mary R. Lefkowitz and Maureen B. Fant, eds., *Women's Life in
   Greece and Rome: A Source Book in Translation.* Baltimore: Johns Hopkins University Press, 1992, pp. 50–51, 53.

9. Seneca, *Consolation of Helvia,* in Moses Hadas, ed. and trans., *The Stoic Philosophy of Seneca.* New York: W.W. Norton, 1958, p. 129.

10. Pliny the Elder, *Natural History,* quoted in Lefkowitz and Fant, *Women's Life
    in Greece and Rome,* pp. 216–17.

11. Juvenal, *Satires,* published as *The Sixteen Satires,* trans. Peter Green. New
    York: Penguin Books, 1974, p. 136.

12. Quoted in Shelton, *As the Romans Did,* p. 63.

13. Sextus Julius Frontinus, *The Aqueducts of Rome,* in *The Stratagems and the
    Aqueducts of Rome,* trans. C.E. Bennett. Cambridge, MA: Harvard University
    Press, 1993, pp. 433–37.

14. Frontinus, *Aqueducts of Rome,* pp. 399, 405.

15. Frontinus, *Aqueducts of Rome,* p. 447.

16. Juvenal, *Satires,* pp. 96–97.

17. Quoted in Shelton, *As the Romans Did,* p. 70.

18. Quoted in Shelton, *As the Romans Did,* p. 71.

19. Quoted in Shelton, *As the Romans Did,* p. 71.

In the Home: Houses and Slaves

Chapter Preface

The noted Roman poet Horace included this fond remembrance in one of his satires: "If my character is . . . decent and moral . . . [and] I live a virtuous life . . . my father deserves all the credit. . . . He deserves from me unstinting gratitude and praise." Like other Roman fathers, Horace's was the paterfamilias, or male leader, of the family, which formed the nucleus of private life and society as a whole. From the father, a young Roman man inherited his name, status, and perhaps property, all essential elements of his identity and social standing. The same can be said for women. This was partially illustrated by the fact that in Horace's day women's names were often feminized forms of one of their fathers' names. (For example, the daughter of Marcus Tullius Cicero was Tullia.)

The family headed by the paterfamilias was more than simply a unit of closely knit relatives, however. In fact, the Latin word for family, *familia,* translates literally as "household," and to the Romans there was more to a household than the core family unit. The home was not only where the children were raised, but also where they were born; where the spirits of beloved ancestors dwelled and influenced the living; and where family members prayed at a home altar (usually set up in some central location, such as a courtyard).

The household was also where young Romans learned firsthand about the strict distinctions in social classes that permeated Roman society. Almost all Roman homes, even a great many of those of lesser financial means, had at least one or two slaves; and some households had five, ten, twenty, or even more slaves. In a way, slaves were seen as part of the family; yet they were also property to be bought, sold, and worked like livestock. Beyond the home, slaves could be found in every niche of Roman society, from the fields to shops and ships, and from the splendor of royal palaces to the dark and dangerous recesses of underground mines. Of all of these slaves, those who lived and worked in households received the best treatment, often enjoying levels of comfort and safety beyond that of poor free Romans.

The homes in which free Romans and their slaves coexisted

varied in size, style, layout, and degree of comforts according to their location and the financial resources of the occupants. In the countryside, most of the people were small farmers who dwelled in modest wooden or stone farmhouses. Their well-to-do neighbors lived in villas, which came in two varieties—that which served as the central focus of a farming estate, and that which was used as a retreat or retirement home. Some examples of the latter were true mansions with all manner of luxuries and large staffs of slaves to maintain them. The famous diplomat and letter-writer Pliny the Younger described his country estate in fascinating detail in a letter that has fortunately survived.

In the cities, by contrast, the majority of Romans lived in rented apartments in large tenement blocks. These usually lacked plumbing and were built with shoddy materials, making them prone to collapse and fire damage. Yet no matter how poor and ramshackle the structure in which a Roman household might be lodged, its members could take pride in being hard-working, moral people and good parents, as attested by Horace. His father was a freedman (freed slave) who worked hard and sacrificed to see that his son received a good education and wore nice clothes. "I could never be ashamed of such a father," Horace wrote, "nor do I feel any need . . . to apologize for being a freedman's son."

Houses and Their Contents

F.R. Cowell

This information-packed overview of Roman townhouses and apartments is by a noted expert on ancient Roman life, F.R. Cowell. Cowell covers not only the physical look of typical homes, but also their heating and lighting devices, furniture, and other common contents. Cowell cites the testimony of a number of contemporary Romans, including two of the first century B.C. (the late Republic)—the orator Cicero and poet Horace; and from the first century A.D. (the early Empire)—the naturalist Pliny the Elder, and the popular satirists Juvenal and Martial.

Just as thousands today, who could live elsewhere, deliberately choose to be in or near London, New York or another great city, so people responded to the lure of Rome. After the first century A.D. there was no comparable city anywhere in the world: Athens and Alexandria undoubtedly had a great deal to offer, but they were much smaller. As the world-centre of political and administrative life, as the source of social distinction, as the creator of new styles and ways of life, Rome was unique. The urge to live in Rome drove up all prices and increased the cost of living. 'In Rome', said Juvenal, 'you have to pay for everything. Everybody dresses above their means, sometimes at someone else's expense. It's a universal failing; we all live here in pretentious poverty.'. . .

Apartments and Town Houses

The difficulty of providing housing for all the people who wanted to live in Rome forced the Romans before Imperial days to adopt the same sort of solution that prevails today in a city such as Paris or New York. Few except the rich could then live in a town house or detached villa. The great majority were housed in blocks of tenements or apartments usually not more than three or four stories high. Early in the Empire, Augustus put a limit of 70 feet on the height of houses because of their rather shoddy construction. The builders probably sought to economise on bricks. As time went on the Romans made much more use of their excellent lime-mortar in building walls and floors. It sets so hard that it has often been mistaken for modern concrete.

By the end of the Republic the wealthy and notable families who owned their own homes were converting them into very elegant mansions. Some were truly palatial, being richly decorated with marble columns, marble floors and walls, and lavishly provided with curtains and elegant furnishings in ivory, bronze and rare woods. Their general plan was the same, a series of rooms built round an inner courtyard or a square or rectangular basin, the *atrium*, and another series of rooms built round an adjoining second courtyard or garden. They seem to have been usually bungalows all on one floor, but sometimes the bedrooms were on a second floor. This form of construction was developed in Republican days. The earlier Roman version of it was the single courtyard with the low roofs of the four sides sloping gently downwards over the courtyard which they did not completely cover but left a gap for rain water to fall into a basin and for smoke to escape from the domestic hearth.

When the Romans became richer they added a second house to this *atrium*. It was on the Greek model and was called the *peristylum*, meaning the part of a building enclosing a courtyard surrounded by columns on the inside. In the larger houses of the rich and in country towns such as Pompeii, this courtyard became a garden. In Rome many of the well-to-do had to be content with roof gardens on a sun-terrace perhaps having fruit trees and fishponds on it. The bedrooms of the family, the domestic shrine, the hearth and kitchen, the dining-room and book store or library, if the owner had any literary interests, were in this *peristylum*. The *atrium* then became the reception hall where the wealthy owner received . . . the stream of his obsequious clients [those who were socially subservient or dependent on them]; its smaller rooms might then be used as offices. The outer walls of such houses were usually without windows, though some had small ones. In a city which, like London, had no police force until quite late in its history, security against marauders was very necessary. The huge doors, bolted and barred and always guarded by slaves and perhaps a fierce dog, are another indication of the need for precautions.

Apart from the houses of the very wealthy on the Palatine Hill, which was increasingly taken over for Imperial palaces during the Empire, and from the villas of the well-to-do on the banks of the Tiber and in suburban areas, the great majority of Roman dwellings were to be found in the apartment and tenement houses in the less fashionable districts of the City. These were strictly utilitarian, mostly made up of small rooms often built over shops and having shuttered windows on the street or on an inner courtyard. Later in the Republic and throughout the Empire, these apartment houses became so large that they filled an 'island' site being bounded on all four sides by streets. Such a block was called an *insula*. Around A.D. 350, a count was made showing that Rome then contained 44,173 *insulae* but only 1,782 private houses (*domus*). Tenants could buy a floor or a room outright, but it was more normal to rent an apartment. Speculative builders and people with money to invest made good incomes by letting rooms, which were not cheap.

After Julius Caesar had returned from the Civil Wars to celebrate his victories in five separate great triumphal processions, it is recorded that he gave 'a year's rent in Rome to tenants who paid 2,000 sesterces or less, and in Italy up to 500 sesterces'. Rents in Rome were therefore about four times as great as in the country. At the same time he gave each of his veteran legionaries 24,000 sesterces 'by way of booty'. The annual interest on that lump sum, if carefully invested, would just about pay a year's rent for a modest room in a cheap apartment house in Rome or it would buy outright a much better home in a country district. 'If you can tear yourself away from the games in the Circus you can buy an excellent house at Sora, at Fabrateria or Frusino for what you now pay in rent for a dingy garret in Rome in one year', said Juvenal. These small towns were near Cicero's birthplace, not more than sixty miles south-east of Rome. Naturally many people paid more than ex-soldiers for larger well-built apartments in a good part of the City, and we hear of rents of 30,000 sesterces a year for a third-floor apartment, which, however, Cicero said was three times as much as it should have been.

Heating, Plumbing, and Sewage Disposal

The convenience of most of the houses and apartments, judged by our standard, was not very great, although there were improvements in the later Empire. It was not until then that even the more palatial houses were well heated. Roman central heating was then achieved by providing spaces under floors and in hollow walls in which the smoke and heat from a fire in a cellar space beneath could circulate. Throughout the Republic and the first and second centuries A.D. Romans had nothing but open charcoal braziers in their rooms so that they suffered considerably in their short sharp winters. Marble walls and stone or marble floors must then have been an affliction to bare feet in sandals. The upper stories had wooden boards. The wealthy contrived to have one of their dining-rooms facing south to benefit from whatever heat the winter sun might give. No rooms, as far as we know, had fireplaces and chimneys except possibly a few kitchens. It was quite late in Imperial days also that thick, opaque glass began to be used for windows. Unless some semi-translucent sheeting of alabaster or other thin material filled the gap, a wooden shutter which blocked out the light was the only way to close a window.

Roman bedrooms seem to have got very stuffy, particularly in winter. Pliny's tip was to disguise the stale smell by burning bread. Water was laid on in lead pipes from the great public aqueducts, but only for the well-to-do, because the users had to pay for it according to the size of their pipes. Martial, who lived a middle class life, said that 'my house complains that it is refreshed by no drop of water although hard-by, the Marcian aqueduct babbles in my ears'. It was not uncommon for Romans to try to escape payment by diverting supplies surreptitiously [secretly] through pipes of their own, sometimes with the connivance of the labourers of the waterworks who were suitably bribed. Sumptuous private houses from the end of the Republic onwards had lavishly decorated bathrooms, so that the rich owner and his family did not need to join the crowds in the public baths, although many did so for the gossip and society they got there. The lavatory seems usually to have been near the kitchen in order to be close to the water supply of the house.

How the tenants in the *insulae* fared in these respects is far from clear. Many probably had to bring water from a fountain and to resort to a common lavatory on the ground floor or to the public lavatories in the streets; and to public baths (a place in which to get warm in winter), just as they had to go to commercial bakeries and cook-shops for bread or hot food. Slops and sewage tipped out of upper windows into the street below was an unpleasant aspect of everyday life in Ancient Rome. . . . 'There's death from every open window as you pass along at night', lamented Juvenal, who said: 'You will be thought a fool if you go out to dinner without having made your will.' 'Look at the height of that towering roof from which a pot cracks my head whenever some broken leaking vessel is pitched out of the window.' Rather than that, 'you pray in terror that they will do no more than empty their slop-pails over you'.

Life was by no means free from fearful risks when the poorer Romans were within the four walls of their tenement rooms. Buildings wear out and in Rome many of them had a notoriously short life because of their shoddy construction. 'We live in a city largely shored up on slender supports', Juvenal complained. Danger from falling buildings was a real obsession. So was the risk of fire. 'The place to live in is where there are no fires', said Juvenal, who knew the perils of cheap lodgings. 'Already your third storey is smoking, you yourself know nothing of it for if the alarm begins at the bottom of the stairs, the last man to know there is a fire will be the one who is protected from the rain only by the roof tiles.'

Furniture and Personal Items

In comparison with modern times, the Romans hardly had any furniture. They lived more as the Japanese do in bare rooms with a minimum of equipment. Changes in the contents of the average Roman house from Republican to Imperial times there certainly were. In the 'Middle Ages' of Rome [i.e., early Republican times]. . . the prized possessions of a Roman would have been, apart from essential clothing and simple frame beds and couches, a collection of rough agricultural implements: spade, mattock, scythe, sickle, hammer, hatchet, knife, rake, hoe and plough, and weapons of war: short sword, shield and lance. Women would have had their spindle, weaving frame, a chair or stool, grinding stones or mill and some rough earthenware and metal cooking utensils. Women's personal knicknacks in these early days would have been few and simple: a comb of wood or bone, a ring and large brooch or two, some bone or metal hair-pins, perhaps a bracelet or two and some ear-rings kept in a simple trinket box made of terra-cotta or boxwood, and a polished metal mirror. The children would have a few simple toys and games.

In the so-called 'Golden Age' of the Roman Empire, some 300–400 years later, the picture would be very different. Gone are the small huts and houses and with them have disappeared the weapons of war and the farmers' tools. To find spindles and weaving frames it would be necessary to look in the slaves' quarters of a few large houses, although here and there one or two families priding themselves on keeping up ancient traditions might still have a few. In the attic hovels and cramped quarters of the poor, nothing would have taken the place of this honourable traditional equipment. Martial, scornful as Romans were of poverty, describes a removal: 'there went along a three-legged truckle bed and a two-legged table and with it a lantern, a bowl and a cracked and leaking chamber-pot. The neck of a flagon was lying under a brazier green with verdigris and there was a stinking jug.' Such, with the addition of some ragged bedcoverings, a few knives and spoons, drinking vessels and perhaps a worn old chest or two, made up the main belongings of thousands of impoverished Romans.

The higher Romans climbed in the social scale, the more they spent on furnishing their homes, but the money did not go so much upon a quantity of possessions as upon better quality goods. 'Your by no means large amount of furniture costs you a million, a pound of silver runs away with five thousand, you buy a gilt coach at the price of a farm, Quintus', said Martial. Fortunes were spent upon small tables of rare wood and ivory of fine design. Cicero spent half a million sesterces on a single table. On the interest alone of such a sum at five per cent, a man like Martial or Juvenal would have lived in modest comfort. . . . Chairs were not the ordinary, everyday affair that they are with us. To be seated was traditionally a matter of dignity and ceremony appropriate to magistrates, to judges and to women. Guests too were invited to be seated as a matter of politeness. Children at school, sedentary workmen such as cobblers, patrons of cheap inns all had small round wooden stools, but in the home, men would usually recline on a couch. Folding stools were, however, common. Chairs with backs and arms were rarer and reserved for women, the aged, and honoured guests. Late in the Republic and throughout the Empire, portable sedan chairs were in general use. Some held two people. Those for ladies were covered until the first century A.D. when conservative opinion was shocked to see some women being carried around in open chairs. . . .

As furniture became more elaborate, beds and couches became more richly decorated, of rare fine wood adorned with ivory, tortoise-shell and gold. The coverings of the rich also became magnificent. Infants had cradles, rocked by a girl slave. Beyond making sure that all their essential equipment of this practical kind was as brightly polished, as beautiful and as elegant as possible, wealthy Romans did not fill their rooms. Some had li-

The majority of Roman citizens lived in crowded apartments and tenement houses, which were often built above shops.

braries but more mundane tastes were mostly in evidence, and resources went into decorations and display. Martial refers to a man with 'an elaborate sideboard loaded with silver and gold plate', to 'crystal cups brought by a fleet from the Nile', to a man whose friends, 'like his pictures and cups, are "genuine antiques"'. Artists were kept busy painting walls of living-rooms and mosaic workers laid floors, often with consummate skill. They were in great demand because the Romans did not cover their floors . . . with carpets. . . .

Lighting a Home

The charcoal-burning braziers, which were the main source of comfort against the cold, were of elegant design and workmanship in richer homes, where the family did not need to congregate round the kitchen hearth—if there was one—on which there were usually some hot embers if not an actual blaze. If the fire went out and the embers were dead, it might be quite a business to get it going again. The first resource would be to beg a flame from a neighbour—then as now, the poor were great borrowers. . . . If that failed it was necessary to produce a spark to light dry tinder, touchwood, leaves or sulphur. Failing a flint and steel, the recipe, according to Pliny, was 'to rub and grate one wood against another, and for this intent there is nothing better than to strike ivy wood with bay'. For light at night, lamps burning olive oil were the stock resource from very early times. They were simple flat saucers of earthenware with a handle at one end and a spout at the other from which a wick emerged made from twisted fibres of flax or papyrus, to hang downwards so that, when lit, its flame would cast light downwards as well as in other directions. . . . In a poor Roman home this expense would have been grudged, for olive oil cost money and it was a food. The more wicks, the better light, but also the greater expense. One of the grand lamps with as many as 14 wicks, would, as Martial says, 'light up an entire feast with its flames', but none but the rich could afford it often. Candles made from tallow fat rolled round a twisted wick were a Roman invention used mainly by the poor, but with careful economy because tallow also could be eaten. . . . A single candle, which is all that many households would afford, gives a poor light, except near the flame. One electric lamp of only 60 watts gives a hundred times as much light. A hundred candles placed around a room nevertheless would be more effective than one such electric lamp, but few Romans could afford so many. . . . All such open-flame lights greatly increased the risk of fires to which Rome was so exposed, but a light was badly needed in the tight-shuttered rooms in which people stumbling about in the dark might have some accident or inadvertently desecrate the little shrine of the household gods. The Romans knew of the existence of crude oil or petroleum, called either *bitumen liquidum* or by its Greek name of *naphtha*, 'which is so very inflammable', said Pliny, 'that nobody makes any use of it'.

Kitchenware and Luxuries

In addition to the rare and costly gold and silver cups, dishes and other vessels adorning the loaded sideboards of the rich, they would own a full service of silver spoons, the Romans' main, if not only, article of tableware, for knives and forks or prongs were used in the kitchen and not at table. Food was eaten with the fingers or with spoons. Small spoons with a sharp-pointed handle were used by guests to extract snails and shell-fish from their shells while their small round bowls at the other end served when eating eggs; larger spoons more akin to our dessertspoons met all requirements for which fingers were inadequate.

At first cups and dishes were mostly of earthenware as none but the rich could afford metal such as bronze, silver and gold, and such luxuries were considered ostentatious [showy]. Romans, like the Greeks, had no word for a plate in the modern sense, hence the need for bread and napkins and slaves with bowls of wine and water and sponges to clean greasy fingers and tables between the courses. Drinking horns were of immemorial antiquity and with the advance of civilisation they became elaborately carved, chased and mounted with silver, gold and gems. Cups of every sort were to be had. . . . All other kinds of earthenware utensils, moulded, engraved and plain, were to be had, as well as those of silver by an ancient Greek master silversmith and the chased and inlaid gold and silver ware of later times, collected and prized by the well-to-do. . . .

During the late Republic and throughout the Empire it would

be in the ladies' apartments rather than in those of their husbands that evidence of great wealth would be most apparent. Golden rings, bracelets, bangles, anklets, ear-rings, pins, buckles, brooches, necklaces, hairpins, fillets lavishly bejewelled and of exquisite workmanship, spilled in lavish profusion from precious caskets which were jewels in themselves. Rows and rows of little pots of alabaster, marble and rare stone contained priceless perfumes and essences. Far outdoing the modest attirements of the middle classes, the gorgeously arrayed women of the richer homes carried personal adornment to heights as great as have ever been known. These aspects of luxurious living are mentioned here although they will again be referred to, because they point to a change of the utmost significance in the Roman way of life, a change that finds illustration in many other aspects of everyday life. It was a change the Romans themselves noticed and many deplored, without however doing anything much to alter their own way of life. Before it happened, Ennius, Rome's first poet, could proudly boast at the end of the third century B.C. in the spartan days of austerity of the Republic: 'Rome stands four-square upon the well-tried way of life of the men of old.' Two hundred years later Horace, looking at the changed manners of the men and women around him, asked 'what does ravaging time not devour?', and said 'our parents' age, worse than our grandfathers', has brought us forth less worthy still, to produce offspring yet more wicked'. So the luxury and refinement in home and furnishings so briefly sketched above have a deeper significance which it will be well to bear in mind. Some efforts were made by more responsible rulers to check the tremendous increase in personal extravagance and luxurious living by laws limiting expenditure on meals, the amount of silver a man should own or the amount of jewellery a woman should wear, but they all failed, for, as Horace summed up the wisdom of ages: 'Of what avail are mere laws if we lack principle?'

A Wealthy Roman Describes His Country Villa

Pliny the Younger

Gaius Plinius Caecilius Secundus, more popularly known as Pliny the Younger (ca. A.D. 61– ca. 113), was a noted Roman government administrator. His large collection of letters survived, providing later ages with an invaluable mine of information about Roman society, especially the private lives of members of the upper classes. The following letter, written to Pliny's friend, Gallus, describes in a fair amount of detail the layout and amenities of his country villa at Laurentum, on the seacoast a few miles south of Ostia, Rome's port city. It is important to keep in mind that Pliny was an extremely rich man who owned other villas and townhouses. And the average Roman did not live in such splendor, which included a heated swimming pool, a ball court, glass doors, and magnificent private views of the ocean. Yet no examination of Roman homes can afford to ignore such mansions; after all, the lifestyles of the rich and famous capture the attention and imagination of people today as much as they did in Pliny's time.

Y ou may wonder why my Laurentine place (or my Laurentian, if you like that better) is such a joy to me, but once you realize the attractions of the house itself, the amenities of its situation, and its extensive seafront, you will have your answer. It is seventeen miles from Rome, so that it is possible to spend the night there after necessary business is done, without having cut short or hurried the day's work, and it can be approached by more than one route; the roads to Laurentum and Ostia both lead in that direction, but you must leave the one at the fourteenth milestone and the other at the eleventh. Whichever way you go, the side road you take is sandy for some distance and

Pliny the Younger, *The Letters of the Younger Pliny*, translated by Betty Radice. New York: Penguin Books, 1969. Copyright © 1969 by Betty Radice. Reproduced by permission.

rather heavy and slow-going if you drive, but soft and easily covered on horseback. The view on either side is full of variety, for sometimes the road narrows as it passes through the woods, and then it broadens and opens out through wide meadows where there are many flocks of sheep and herds of horses and cattle driven down from the mountains in winter to grow sleek on the pastures in the springlike climate.

Designed to Let in the Sun

The house is large enough for my needs but not expensive to keep up. It opens into a hall, unpretentious but not without dignity, and then there are two colonnades [rows of columns], rounded like the letter D, which enclose a small but pleasant courtyard. This makes a splendid retreat in bad weather, being protected by windows and still more by the overhanging roof. Opposite the middle of it is a cheerful inner hall, and then a dining-room which really is rather fine: it runs out towards the shore, and whenever the sea is driven inland by the south-west wind it is lightly washed by the spray of the spent breakers. It has folding doors or windows as large as the doors all round, so that at the front and sides it seems to look out on to three seas, and at the back has a view through the inner hall, the courtyard with the two colonnades, and the entrance-hall to the woods and mountains in the distance.

To the left of this and a little farther back from the sea is a large bedroom, and then another smaller one which lets in the morning sunshine with one window and holds the last rays of the evening sun with the other; from this window too is a view of the sea beneath, this time at a safe distance. In the angle of this room and the dining-room is a corner which retains and intensifies the concentrated warmth of the sun, and this is the winter-quarters and gymnasium of my household for no winds can be heard there except those which bring the rain clouds, and the place can still be used after the weather has broken. Round the corner is a room built round in an apse to let in the sun as it moves round and shines in each window in turn, and with one wall fitted with shelves like a library to hold the books which I read and read again. Next comes a bedroom on the other side of a passage which has a floor raised and fitted with pipes to receive hot steam and circulate it at a regulated temperature. The remaining rooms on this side of the house are kept for the use of my slaves and freedmen, but most of them are quite presentable enough to receive guests.

On the other side of the dining-room is an elegantly decorated bedroom, and then one which can either be a bedroom or a moderate-sized dining-room and enjoys the bright light of the sun reflected from the sea; behind is another room with an antechamber, high enough to be cool in summer and a refuge in winter, for it is sheltered from every wind. A similar room and antechamber are divided off by a single wall. Then comes the cooling-room of the bath, which is large and spacious and has two

A Farming Villa

The country villa Pliny describes was mainly a retreat he used to get away from the hustle and bustle of the city. Another common kind of villa was the farming villa, which served as the central focus of a well-to-do farming estate. This description of a farming villa is by Lucius Junius Columella, a first-century A.D. estate owner who wrote a handbook about farming.

The size of a villa or housing structure should be determined by the total area of the farm; and the villa should be divided into three sections: one section resembling a city home [for the landowner], one section like a real farmhouse [for the workers and livestock], and the third section for storing farm products.

The landowner's section of the villa should be further divided into a winter apartment and a summer apartment. The winter bedrooms should face southeast and the winter dining rooms due west. The summer bedrooms, on the other hand, should face due south, but the dining rooms for this same season should face southeast. The baths should be turned toward the northwest so that they may be lighted from midday until evening. The promenades should have a southern exposure so that they may receive both the maximum of sun in the winter and the minimum in the summer.

Now in the farmhouse part of the villa there should be a large kitchen with a high ceiling, and for two reasons: so that the wood beams may be secure against the danger of fire, and so that household slaves may conveniently stop by here during every season of the year. The best plan will be to construct the cells for unchained slaves facing south. For those in chains let there be an underground prison, as healthful as possible, and let it be lighted by many narrow curved baths built out of opposite walls; these are quite large enough if you consider that the sea is so near. Next come the oiling-room, the furnace-room, and the antechamber to the bath, and then two rest-rooms, beautifully decorated in a simple style, leading to the heated swimming-bath which is much admired and from which swimmers can see the sea. Close by is the ball-court which receives the full warmth of the setting sun. Here there is a second storey, with two living-rooms below and two above, as well as a dining-room which commands the whole expanse of sea and stretch of shore with all its lovely houses. Elsewhere another upper storey contains a room which receives both the rising and setting sun, and a good-sized wine-store and granary behind,

---

windows which are built so far from the ground that they cannot be reached with a hand. . . .

The third part of the villa, that designated for storing produce, is divided into rooms for oil, for oil and wine presses, for aged wine, and for wine not yet fermented; into lofts for hay and straw; and into areas for warehouses and granaries. The rooms which are on the ground floor serve to store liquid products, such as wine and olive oil, which are destined for the market; however, dry products, such as grain, hay, leaves, straw, and other fodders, should be stored in lofts. The granaries should be reached by ladders and should receive ventilation through tiny little openings on the north wall. For that direction is the most cold and the least humid, two factors which contribute to a long preservation for stored grain. For the same reason, the wine room is placed on the ground floor; but it should be far removed from the bathrooms, the oven, the manure pile, and other filthy areas giving off a foul stench, and just as far from cisterns and running water that release a liquid which spoils the wine. . . .

The rooms for wine and oil presses especially, and the storerooms for olive oil, should be warm because every liquid is more readily thinned by heat, but thickened by great cold; and if the oil freezes (which seldom happens), it becomes rancid. But, as it is natural heat which is needed—heat which depends on the position of the sun and the angle of its rays—fire and flames are unnecessary, since the flavor of the oil is spoiled by smoke and soot. Therefore the press room should receive sun from the south so that we do not find it necessary to use fires and lamps when the olives are being pressed.

Quoted in Jo-Ann Shelton, ed. and trans., *As The Romans Did: A Source Book in Roman Social History.* New York: Oxford University Press, 1988, pp. 73–75.

while below is a dining-room where nothing is known of a high
sea but the sound of the breakers, and even that as a dying murmur; it looks on to the garden and the encircling drive.

The Grounds

All round the drive runs a hedge of box [a variety of evergreen
tree], or rosemary to fill any gaps, for box will flourish exten-
sively where it is sheltered by the buildings, but dries up if exposed in the open to the wind and salt spray even at a distance.
Inside the inner ring of the drive is a young and shady vine per-
gola, where the soil is soft and yielding even to the bare foot. The
garden itself is thickly planted with mulberries and figs, trees
which the soil bears very well though it is less kind to others. On
this side the dining-room away from the sea has a view as lovely
as that of the sea itself, while from the windows of the two
rooms behind can be seen the entrance to the house and another
well-stocked kitchen garden.

Here begins a covered arcade nearly as large as a public building. It has windows on both sides, but more facing the sea, as
there is one in each alternate bay on the garden side. These all
stand open on a fine and windless day, and in stormy weather
can safely be opened on the side away from the wind. In front is
a terrace scented with violets. As the sun beats down, the arcade
increases its heat by reflection and not only retains the sun but
keeps off the north-east wind so that it is as hot in front as it is
cool behind. In the same way it checks the south-west wind, thus
breaking the force of winds from wholly opposite quarters by one
or the other of its sides; it is pleasant in winter but still more so
in summer when the terrace is kept cool in the morning and the
drive and nearer part of the garden in the afternoon, as its
shadow falls shorter or longer on one side or the other while the
day advances or declines. Inside the arcade, of course, there is
least sunshine when the sun is blazing down on its roof, and as
its open windows allow the western breezes to enter and circulate, the atmosphere is never heavy with stale air.

The Private Suite

At the far end of the terrace, the arcade and the garden is a suite
of rooms which are really and truly my favourites, for I had them

built myself. Here is a sun-parlour facing the terrace on one side, the sea on the other, and the sun on both. There is also a room which has folding doors opening on to the arcade and a window looking out on the sea. Opposite the intervening wall is a beautifully designed alcove which can be thrown into the room by folding back its glass doors and curtains, or cut off from it if they are closed: it is large enough to hold a couch and two arm-chairs, and has the sea at its foot, the neighbouring villas behind, and the woods beyond, views which can be seen separately from its many windows or blended into one. Next to it is a bedroom for use at night which neither the voices of my household, the sea's murmur, nor the noise of a storm can penetrate, any more than the lightning's flash and light of day unless the shutters are open. This profound peace and seclusion are due to the dividing passage which runs between the room and the garden so that any noise is lost in the intervening space. A tiny furnace-room is built on here, and by a narrow outlet retains or circulates the heat underneath as required. Then there is an ante-room and a second bedroom, built out to face the sun and catch its rays the moment it rises, and retain them until after midday, though by then at an angle. When I retire to this suite I feel as if I have left my house altogether and much enjoy the sensation: especially during the Saturnalia [a religious holiday celebrated in December] when the rest of the roof resounds with festive cries in the holiday freedom, for I am not disturbing my household's merrymaking nor they my work.

Nearby Amenities

Only one thing is needed to complete the amenities and beauty of the house—running water; but there are wells, or rather springs, for they are very near the surface. It is in fact a remarkable characteristic of this shore that wherever you dig you come upon water at once which is pure and not in the least brackish, although the sea is so near. The woods close by provide plenty of firewood, and the town of Ostia supplies us with everything else. There is also a village, just beyond the next house, which can satisfy anyone's modest needs, and here there are three baths for hire, a great convenience if a sudden arrival or too short a stay makes us reluctant to heat up the bath at home. The seafront gains much from the pleasing variety of the houses built either in groups or far apart; from the sea or shore these look like a number of cities. The sand on the shore is sometimes too soft for walking after a long spell of fine weather, but more often it is hardened by the constant washing of the waves. The sea has admittedly few fish of any value, but it gives us excellent soles and prawns, and all inland produce is provided by the house, especially milk: for the herds collect there from the pastures whenever they seek water and shade.

And now do you think I have a good case for making this retreat my haunt and home where I love to be? You are too polite a townsman if you don't covet it! But I hope you will, for then the many attractions of my treasured house will have another strong recommendation in your company.

Slavery in Roman Society

Michael Grant

Slavery was the largest and most entrenched social institution in ancient Rome (especially at its height, between 200 B.C. and A.D. 200) and affected every aspect of life and society. This informative overview of Roman slavery is by noted University of Edinburgh scholar Michael Grant. He cites numerous ancient writers, among them the Roman jurist Gaius, the Roman playwright Plautus, the Romanized Greek historian Appian, the great Roman historian Tacitus, the Roman naturalist and encyclopedist Pliny the Elder, and Columella, a Roman gentleman who wrote a long book about how to manage a farming estate. Grant is careful to explain how the slavery institution, as well as attitudes toward slaves, changed over the centuries; in Rome's last centuries, for example, the need for slaves lessened somewhat as many free Romans became serfs, poor farm workers dependent on wealthy landowners. Yet slavery persisted right up to Rome's fall. As Grant points out, when the Christians finally gained control of Rome, they made no effort to abolish slavery, although most Christians did advocate humane treatment of slaves.

In Rome . . . the slave was not a person but a property; the legal writer Gaius tells us so, adding that the distinction between free man and slave is fundamental. They had no status in the civil law. . . . The Romans did not write much about it [slavery], in depth. But the strong sense of property in Roman law is partly, or largely, derived from slave ownership.

In early Rome, slavery developed within the framework of the family. As in Greece, the existence and possession of slaves helped free Romans to engage in their various occupations, such as politics; and enabled them, too, to show off their wealth. People were afraid of slaves, and their treatment varied widely. They

Michael Grant, *A Social History of Greece and Rome*. New York: Charles Scribner's Sons, 1992.

could be looked after decently—and form a respected part of the household—or they might be tortured, and thrown to wild beasts, and sexually abused, and have their families broken up by sale: in fact they could be treated very cruelly indeed. A slave was not allowed to dispose of his property as he wished, but he could own property, his *peculium* or private savings (to which he could add), and the legal recognition of this practice was something that had never existed in Greece. It gave slaves greater independence of action, and they carried on a lot of business at Rome, acting on their own account. Indeed, their prominence in these fields helped to degrade industry and trade in people's minds.

A Society Dependent on Slaves

Rome can be called a society largely dependent on slaves from the third century B.C. onwards. During the Second Punic War (218–201) various developments occurred. First, military operations resulted in large-scale enslavements. Secondly, and exceptionally, slaves were called upon to fight, and were bought for the purpose. Thirdly, with so many free men away in the army, the role of slaves on the home front became more and more significant: they were employed in agricultural and industrial production on an unprecedented scale, without which the free recruits for the army could never have been raised and taken away. Conscious of their new powers, some slaves made trouble, especially in Campania [the fertile region near the Bay of Naples]. As a . . . safety-valve, they were allowed religious activities, and, in particular, played a dramatic role in the annual Saturnalia, transformed into a Greek-style festival, in which slaves momentarily changed places with their masters—the compliment being intended to prompt future loyalty among the slaves, by showing gratitude for the work they were doing.

But free people were still really afraid of their slaves, as the plays of Plautus, despite comic exaggeration and irony, make clear. His slaves have much larger roles than those of Menander's Greek New Comedy on which he drew: male slaves are crafty and resourceful, and their female counterparts (on whose child-bearing the future of the institution partly depended) are ubiquitous [present in large numbers].

Cato the elder, in his *On Agriculture*, was probably more liberal than many of his contemporaries. But he regarded slaves as basically intractable, and went into somewhat chilling, pragmatic [practical] details about how they ought to be handled. It was only common sense, he said, that, like pieces of equipment, they should be cared for, but not as carefully as oxen, which could not look after themselves. Old and decrepit slaves might have their rations reduced and could be sold off, like worn-out tools or aged oxen or 'anything else that is superfluous'. . . .

Cato's detailed comments, even if they sound damping, were timely, because from the end of the Second Punic War until the end of the Republic there was a dramatic increase of both urban and rural slavery in Italy. This was partly because of the influx of slaves during the eastern wars of conquest (augmented by piracy), which . . . opened the way to the huge importation of slaves into Italian agriculture—including the large senatorial estates—and into manufacture and profitable state mines (at the expense, very often, of the free poor). The growth in the population of Rome itself, too, provided a large market for the new surplus provided by the slaves. As a result of all this, by the time of Caesar's death—although all statistics are dubious—it seems quite probable that one-third of Italy's total population of six or seven million were slaves, as against 10 per cent before the Second Punic War.

The Slave Rebellions

So the slaves, or some of them—not surprisingly—had begun to feel their strength, and express their discontents by forcible means. There were Italian slave risings in 198, 196 and 185 B.C. Then there were three great revolts during periods of severe social strain, the first two in Sicily (*c.* 139–132 and 104–100), and the third led by Spartacus in south Italy (73–71). Although their frequency and scale have been overemphasised, they were serious enough. But they were not . . . ideological manifestations of a 'class struggle', directed at the universal abolition of slavery— on the contrary, Eunus of Apamea, leader of the first revolt, had an imposing slave retinue himself—but responses to specific injustices, by specific groups of slaves in special circumstances, who objected, or whose leaders objected, to being ill-treated, and wanted to take revenge on their masters, or to get away. . . .

Eunus's only programme was to seize Sicily for himself, and

rule it as a sort of Hellenistic monarchy. . . . He appealed to religion and the divine world, and magic, for help. . . .

As for Spartacus, he has been overestimated . . . encouraged by the exaggerations of his contemporary Roman enemy Crassus, who wanted to build him up as a worthy foe. It was ludicrous to describe Spartacus as a 'precursor of social revolution' or 'the leader of a unified proletarian resistance front'. He started with 200 gladiators, of whom 78 made a successful break. The product of local conditions and scattered support (not including town slaves), he did not lead any lower-class unity movement, but tried to break out and return with a group of his own followers, in the hope of leading them back to Thrace, the land of his origin. What he wanted to do was not to lead a universal lower-class movement, but to fight in order to get his men back to their homelands.

All the slave revolts ended in failure, because the slaves were not powerful or unified enough to succeed. Republican society was cracking up for other reasons, but not because of the slave rebellions. More than a million slaves had been killed in the course of the fighting, and the slave-owners were not even dented. On the contrary, under the late Republic, the quantitative employment of slave labour reached its high-water mark in ancient history. Crassus possessed a vast number. A proposal that slaves should wear distinctive clothing was rejected, because it would have shown how numerous they were. Most were still obtained as prisoners of war. Although, on the whole, they were treated even worse than before, the potentialities of all these slaves as political supporters and pressure groups did not escape the notice of Roman public figures, so that slaves were now allowed to contract *contubernia* (nearly marriages) and their family life was, on occasion, encouraged, and they could attend *collegia* [clubs, such as those that helped arrange the funerals of members], in which they met free members of the community. Politicians who wanted to defy the senate often called on slaves to help them (usually without success). . . .

Changing Attitudes About Slaves

As Appian pointed out, the Civil Wars after Caesar's death gave slaves not only . . . a share of their masters' power, but even power over their masters, whom many of them saved during the proscription era [the years when powerful leaders were murdering their political opponents]. . . . It was therefore thought advisable to give some of them rewards and privileges. The question arose of arming them in the current conflicts. It was considered criminal to do so, and the worst offender, according to Octavian (Augustus), was his enemy Sextus Pompeius, who enlisted runaway slaves; Octavian described his war against Sextus as a 'slave war' (*bellum servorum*). There followed a vast number of western enslavements after Octavian had won his civil wars, and became Augustus. Augustus also introduced a radical constitutional change, stressing state interference in slave-owners' rights over their slaves—who could now, even, inform against their masters. He also restricted the use of torture to extract evidence from them.

From then onwards the importation of slaves somewhat decreased, since wars of conquest, on the whole, diminished, and so did piracy. But slave-breeding largely filled the gap—with the assistance of disreputable professional slave-catchers—and there is no direct evidence for a decline in total slave numbers; probably the demand remained constant until the end of the second century A.D. Some slave households were enormous. Gaius Caelius Isidorus . . . left 4,116 slaves. . . . In the time of Augustus, it has been estimated, there were about 300,000 slaves at Rome, out of a total population of about one million. Many of them were small traders, among whom slaves were more numerous than free men.

There was a good deal of early imperial law-making to protect slaves, but it was not usually as humanitarian as it was made to look, since it was often a continuation of Augustus's policy of asserting state control. A senatorial decree under Claudius was directed against the marriages of free women to slaves—reducing the women to slave status themselves; a measure, incidentally, which reveals that such marital relationships existed on a not inconsiderable scale.

Yet, at the same time, a humane attitude to slaves was undeniably on the increase. For it was realised that they should not be too freely expendable—should, that is to say, receive better treatment—and the increasing number of home-bred slaves seemed to require more careful consideration, not least because it involved personal friendships with their masters and their masters' families. There were also two imperial training schools for slave boys which ensured many of them a proper education.

Besides, Stoic, cosmopolitan feelings were at work. They are particularly apparent in the writings of Seneca the younger, who offered our only detailed and thorough exposition of the relationship between masters and slaves, who ought, he declared . . . , to be decently treated. . . .

It is possible to be a little cynical about his pronouncements, because he was not really abolitionist. . . . Yet his contribution does show that liberal views were in the air—and he may well, to some extent, have shared them. In any case, he mirrored what was evidently a certain unease.

Fear of Slaves Was Strong

For certainly, in Seneca's time, there was an increasing recognition of the *moral* personality of slaves. Besides, in some ways a Roman domestic slave was better off than a poor freeman. This was most conspicuously the case in the astonishing phenomenon of the imperial household (*familia Caesaris*). Most of its leading members . . . were freedmen, but they also included unfreed slaves holding highly lucrative and influential posts at court, at Rome particularly. . . but also in imperial offices elsewhere. Thus Musicus Scurranus, a mere cashier (*dispensator*) in one of the provincial treasuries of Tiberius (A.D. 14–37), was very rich, owning much silver plate, and had at least sixteen household slaves of his own, who dedicated a monument in his honour. . . .

But a limit to this interpenetration of classes had to be drawn somewhere, to placate senatorial opinion; and that was probably why Claudius, as we have seen, restricted the marriages of these slaves with free women. For feeling against slaves, and fear of them, in leading circles was still strong. A classic case arose in A.D. 61 when the city prefect of Rome, Lucius Pedanius Secundus, was murdered by one of his 400 slaves. 'After the murder,' recounts Tacitus, 'ancient custom required that every slave residing under the same roof must be executed. But a crowd gathered, eager to save so many innocent lives; and rioting began. The senate house was besieged. Inside, there was feeling against excessive severity. But the majority opposed any change.'

And one of their number, Gaius Cassius Longinus, made a long and eloquent speech. . . urging that the mass executions should be carried out to the letter. 'Our ancestors', he is reported as saying, 'distrusted their slaves. Yet slaves were then born on the same estates, in the same houses, as their masters, who had treated them kindly from birth. But nowadays our huge households are international. They include every alien religion—or none at all. The only way to keep down this scum is by intimidation. Innocent people will die, you say. Yes, and when in a defeated army every tenth man is flogged to death, the brave have to draw lots with the others. Exemplary punishment always contains an element of injustice. But individual wrongs are outweighed by the advantage of the community.' Cassius Longinus, echoing the fears and anxieties of many Romans, had his way, and the dead man's slaves, men, women and children alike, were taken off for execution. But in view of the outcry among the rest of the population (so many of whom were descended from slaves), Nero [the current emperor] had to line the whole route, along which they were taken, with troops.

So the slaves prompted fear, but also prompted sympathy; and one can trace two main elements in current thinking in many contemporary and later writers, who did not go into the matter as deeply as Seneca, but nevertheless made interesting passing remarks. The elder Pliny describes slave field-workers in Italy as 'men without hope', and does not believe that they work as well as free men. Columella, on the other hand, for practical reasons, recommends favourable treatment for slavewomen who produced children. By producing four, they had repaid their purchase price.

And he had similar practical considerations to apply to the treatment of slave-overseers:

> My advice at the start is not to appoint a [farm] overseer from that sort of slaves who are physically attractive. . . .
>
> He should be given a woman companion to keep him within bounds and yet in certain matters to be a help to him. And this same overseer should be warned not to become intimate with a member of the household, and much less with an outsider. . . .

But meanwhile attention was being directed towards slaves'

personal contributions to culture. Two second-century authors devoted themselves to this theme. Gellius gave a list of philosophers who had been slaves. And Hermippus of Berytus wrote *On Slaves Famous in the Cultural Domain.* According to antique tradition the role of the slave had been that of the *paedagogus,* who looked after the children and took them to school. But ever since Republican days they had also provided teachers. There were also slave doctors, and doctors' assistants, and nurses. Doctors for the Romans, slaves and freedmen, had been imported from Greece since the second century B.C., and free-born doctors employed slave doctors to help them. Greek physicians were not always well regarded, and one reason why the medical profession stood in low repute was because it recruited slaves (of an advanced age). . . .

No Abolition Under the Christians

After about A.D. 200 there was a decline in the number of slaves in the Roman empire, though it came about slowly, and was perhaps not as large as was formerly thought. The slave population, in the long run, did not reproduce itself: and the . . . reduction of many men to serfdom meant that the same quantity of slaves was no longer necessary, or profitable. Or at least not everywhere: because in the fourth century . . . every wealthy home was still full of Gothic or Scythian slaves. . . .

And people still felt they had to be on guard against them. An Edict of Diocletian (284–305) had shown awareness of this. In the time of Constantine I the Great (306–337), an appeal was made to their feelings by a law that the murder of a slave and a free man were equally serious crimes, with the same penalties. Constantine also thought it reasonable that slave families should not be divided:

> When . . . estates in Sardinia were recently distributed among the various present proprietors, the division of holdings ought to have been made in such a way that a whole family of slaves would remain with one individual land-holder. For who could tolerate that children should be separated from parents, sisters from brothers, and wives from husbands?

Nevertheless, discontent among slaves continued, and although it did not bring about the fall of the western empire . . . it did nothing to prevent the process. For the various 'peasant' revolts of the time, which helped to undermine the imperial régime, attracted slave supporters: a wealthy landowner in the hands of the rebel Bagaudae in Gaul became the slave of his own slaves. Moreover, slaves were attracted to the causes of invading barbarians. Out of the 40,000 people who escaped from Rome to the Visigoth Alaric's camp in 408–409 a large number were people of slave status. And in 417 we learn that a town in Gaul was handed over to the barbarians by what was described as a slave faction (*factio servilis*).

When the empire had become Christian under Constantine, despite the humanitarian legislation of the time (which was not specifically Christian), the event made little impact on slavery as a practical phenomenon. Jesus, in his parables, had seen the slave's subjection as a symbol of the relation between man and God. And Paul did not harbour the runaway slave Onesimus, but instead tried to persuade him to return to his Christian master Philemon. When he says that 'there is no such thing as . . . slave and free-man', he is talking in a spiritual sense, and pointing out that they are equal in the sight of God. But, in earthly terms, he exhorts them to be obedient, and obey their masters: he is anxious that Christianity should present no scandal to the eyes of the authorities.

True, slaves, like women, figured largely in early Christian society—and they were comforted by the insidious theory, which had originated so many centuries earlier, that the good and wise person was never 'really' a slave. St Jerome, it is true, was critical of the institution in one, moral respect—seeing domestic slavery as a peril to household virtue. And Augustine recognised that the system was evil in principle. Yet he saw no alternative to accepting it. Indeed he and Ambrose felt that slavery could actually be good for the slave, who would earn a special reward, in the afterlife, for the disadvantages he had suffered and overcome on earth.

A Roman Calls for Kinder Treatment of Slaves

Seneca the Younger

While some Romans were strict or even harsh with their slaves, others treated them very humanely, sometimes as members of the family. Among those in the second group was Seneca the Younger, an urbane philosopher, playwright, and adviser to the emperor Nero in the mid–first century A.D. Much of Seneca's attitude about slaves stemmed from the fact that he was a Stoic. Stoicism was a philosophical movement that became very popular among Roman intellectuals, especially in the first and second centuries A.D. According to its main doctrines, the cosmos is endowed with divine purpose or intelligence (*logos*), a tiny spark of divine fire existing in every human. Therefore, all people, from wealthy aristocrats to lowly slaves, are spiritual brothers. (Still, neither Seneca nor any other Stoic went so far as to advocate actually abolishing slavery, which all agreed was the will of the gods.) This statement about the treatment of slaves comes from a letter Seneca wrote to his friend Lucilius. The tract is instructive because, while advocating humane treatment, Seneca describes many common examples of *in*humane treatment of slaves in his society.

Your attitude to your slaves is one of familiarity, as I learn from people who have been in your company. I am pleased; it is what one expects of your good sense and cultivation. "They are slaves"—no, men. "They are slaves"—no, comrades. "They are slaves"—no, humble friends. "They are slaves"—no, fellow slaves, if you remember that Fortune holds equal sway over both.

That is why I laugh at people who think it degrading for a man to dine with his slave. Why, except that conventional exclusiveness has decreed that a master must be surrounded at his dinner by a squad of slaves standing at attention? The master eats more than he can hold; his inordinate greed loads his distended belly, which has unlearned the belly's function, and the digestion of all this food requires more ado than its ingestion. But the unhappy slaves may not move their lips for so much as a word. Any murmur is checked by a rod; not even involuntary sounds—a cough, a sneeze, a choke—are exempted from the lash. If a word breaks the silence the penalty is severe. Hungry and mute, they stand through the whole night.

In consequence, when they cannot speak in the master's presence, they speak *about* him. Yet when slaves spoke not only in the master's presence but *with* him, when their lips were not sewn tight, they were ready to put their necks out for their master, to turn any danger that threatened him upon their own heads; they spoke at dinners, but under torture their lips were sealed. But afterward the arrogance of masters gave currency to the proverb, "So many slaves, so many enemies." We do not acquire them as enemies, we make them such. Other cruel and inhuman treatment I pass over: we abuse them as one does pack animals, not even as one abuses men. When we recline at table one slave wipes up the hawking [spit], another crouches to take up the leavings of the drunks. One carves the costly game, separating the portions by deft sweeps of a practiced hand—unhappy man, to live solely for the purpose of carving fowl neatly, unless the man who teaches the trade for pleasure's sake is more wretched than the man who learns it for necessity's!. . . Another has the assignment of keeping book on the guests; he stands there, poor fellow, and watches to see whose adulation and whose intemperance of gullet or tongue will get him an invitation for the following day. Add the caterers with their refined *expertise* of the master's palate; they know what flavors will titillate him, what table decorations will please his fancy, what novelty might restore his appetite when he feels nauseous . . . what tidbit he would crave on a particular day. With slaves like these the master cannot bear to dine; he would count it an affront to his dignity to come to table with his own slave. Heaven forbid!. . .

Remember, if you please, that the man you call slave sprang from the same seed, enjoys the same daylight, breathes like you, lives like you, dies like you. You can as easily conceive him a free man as he can conceive you a slave. In the Marian disasters many men of noble birth who had entered military service as the preliminary to a senatorial career were declassed by Fortune and reduced to being shepherds or cottagers; now despise a man for his condition when you may find yourself in the same even as you despise it!

I do not wish to take up the large topic of the treatment of slaves, where we show ourselves proud, cruel, and insulting in the highest degree. The essence of my teaching is this: Treat your inferior as you would wish your superior to treat you. Whenever the thought of your wide power over your slave strikes you, be struck, too, by the thought of your master's equally wide power over you. "But I have no master!" you object. All in good time; you may have one. Remember how old Hecuba was when she became a slave, or Croesus, or Darius' mother, or Plato, or Diogenes.

Treat your slave with compassion, even with courtesy; admit

Slaves wait to be sold on a Roman auction block. Although he did not support abolition, Seneca did advocate the humane treatment of slaves.

him to your conversation, your planning, your society. Here the genteel will protest loudly and unanimously: "Nothing could be more degrading or disgusting!" But these same people I shall catch kissing the hands of other people's slaves. Can't you see how our ancestors stripped the title of master of all invidiousness [unpleasantness] and the title of slave of all contumely [insolence]? The master they called "paterfamilias" and the slaves "family"; this usage still obtains in the mimes [comedic sketches performed by street actors]. They instituted a festival at which masters dined with their slaves [the Saturnalia, celebrated in December]—not, of course, the only day they could do so. They allowed slaves to hold office in the household and to act as judges; the household they regarded as a miniature republic.

Judge Them by Their Character

"What is the upshot? Am I to bring all slaves to my table?" No more than all free men. But if you imagine I would exclude some because their work is dirty, that muleteer, for example, or that cowhand, you are mistaken. I value them not by their jobs but by their character; a man gives himself his own character, accident allots his job. Have some dine with you because they are deserving, some to make them deserving. If their sordid contacts have left a taint, association with respectable people will shake it off. There is no reason to go to the forum or senate house in search of a friend, my dear Lucilius; if you pay careful heed you will find one at home. Without an artisan good material often lies unused; try it and you will find out.

A man is a fool if he looks only at the saddle and bridle and not at the horse itself when he is going to buy one; he is a greater fool if he values a man by his clothing and condition, which only swathes us like clothing. "He is a slave!" But perhaps a free man in spirit. "He is a slave!" Shall that count against him? Show me a man who is not; one is a slave to lust, another to greed, another to ambition, all to fear. I can show you a consular [government official] who is slave to a crone [an old woman, i.e., his mother], a millionaire who is slave to a housemaid; I can point to young aristocrats indentured to pantomimes. Voluntary slavery is the meanest of all.

Those squeamish types should not deter you, therefore, from

camaraderie with your slaves and make you proudly superior. Slaves ought to respect rather than fear you. Here someone will protest that I am now rallying slaves to the cap of liberty and toppling masters from their elevation by saying, "Slaves ought to respect rather than fear a master." "That is what he said: slaves ought to respect him, like his clients or those who pay him formal calls." The protester forgets that what is enough for a god is not too little for a master. If a man is respected he is also loved, and love cannot blend with fear.

Your own attitude is consequently as right as can be, in my judgment; you do not choose to have your slaves fear you, you use words to castigate [punish] them. A lash is to admonish dumb beasts. What offends need not wound. It is our daintiness that drives us to distraction, so that anything that does not meet our caprice provokes our wrath. We assume regal lordliness. Kings forget their own strength and others' weakness and fly into a white-hot fury as if they had really been injured, when their exalted position guarantees them complete immunity to any possibility of injury. Nor are they unaware of their immunity; by complaining, they solicit an opening for inflicting harm. They profess they have been injured in order to work injury.

I do not wish to detain you longer; you need no exhortation [encouragement]. Among its other traits good character approves its decisions and abides by them. Wickedness is fickle and changes frequently, not for something better but for something different. Farewell.

In Society: Religion, Weddings, and Roads

Chapter Preface

Rome was a densely crowded city, and for the average person who lacked the luxury of being carried in a covered litter, venturing out in public at midday could be a daunting experience. "Although we hurry," the first-century satirist Juvenal wrote, "we are blocked by a wave of people in front of us. And the great crowd behind crushes us. One man hits me with his elbow, another with a hard pole. . . . My legs are covered with thick mud. Then, on all sides, big feet step on me, and a nail from a soldier's boot pierces my toe."

The fact is that the inhabitants of Rome could not avoid crowds, in part because most of them were social animals who regularly gathered in public for a wide variety of reasons. There was business to attend to, of course, in the busy marketplaces and in the courts. Large groups of people also gathered to listen to orators in the Forum, or to enjoy communal bathing in facilities that could accommodate thousands of patrons at once.

In addition, public games such as chariot races and gladiatorial bouts, as well as religious festivals and celebrations, drew huge crowds. At the religious festivals, worshipers thronged around altars set up outside the temples and either watched or participated in public sacrifice of various animals to honor and also nourish the gods. A few of these ceremonies were recorded by Roman writers, including the novelist Apuleius's account of the high point of a festival honoring Isis, a goddess who originated in Egypt.

Still other occasions in which large numbers of people gathered were wedding ceremonies and receptions. These festive congregations of people contained much formal ritual, as is true of modern weddings, including the transference of the bride from her parents' home and legal protection to her husband's. A number of feasts were also held and the participants sang songs dedicated to the god of weddings so that he would look kindly on the new marriage union.

The crowds at such gatherings were not always strictly local in makeup. Both religious festivals and wedding celebrations, as well as some public games and other communal activities, often drew people from faraway regions and towns. Their travels, along with commercial trade and the movement of Roman armies to trouble spots or frontier forts, would have been severely hampered without Rome's magnificent system of roads. Thousands of miles of roads, both paved and unpaved, crisscrossed the Roman realm, creating a social, commercial, communications, and engineering network that remained unmatched anywhere in the world until modern times.

In fact, the road system was such a well-made, convenient means of travel that it attracted some of the idle well-to-do, who might be described as the ancient version of modern jet-setters. "Some people," the playwright Seneca pointed out, "undertake aimless journeys and wander up and down the coast. An unhealthy restlessness always afflicts them wherever they are." For the most part such wayfarers enjoyed the uncrowded open spaces along the roads. But then, after boredom set in, came the inevitable call: "Let's go back to Rome!"; and as they approached the city, where many roads converged, they encountered the same crowded conditions Juvenal described. As remains true today, if one wants the social, business, and entertainment opportunities afforded by the city, one must learn to put up with crowds.

Roman Religious Beliefs and Practices

Antony Kamm

In this comprehensive summary, scholar Antony Kamm of the University of Stirling explains a wide range of aspects of ancient Roman religion. These include the origins of Roman spiritual beliefs (including the influence of the Etruscans, an early people who lived in Etruria, the region north of Rome), prayer and sacrifice, divination (the interpretation of natural signs, or omens, to foretell the future), household spirits, the colleges (organizations of priests), the *pontifex maximus* (chief state priest), the growth of Eastern mystery religions (which offered the promise of salvation after death), and the ultimate rise of Christianity.

The Romans had a pragmatic attitude to religion, as to most things, which perhaps explains why they themselves had difficulty in taking to the idea of a single, all-seeing, all-powerful god. In so far as they had a religion of their own . . . it was not based on any central belief, but on a mixture of fragmented rituals, taboos, superstitions, and traditions which they collected over the years from a number of sources. To the Romans, religious faith was less a spiritual experience than a contractual relationship between mankind and the forces which were believed to control people's existence and well-being. The result was essentially two-fold: a state cult whose significant influence on political and military events outlasted the Republic, and a private concern, in which the head of the family supervised the domestic rituals and prayers in the same way as the elected representatives of the people performed the public ceremonials. As circumstances and man's view of the world changed, individuals whose personal religious needs remained unsatisfied turned increasingly during the first century AD to the mysteries, which were of Greek origin, and to the cults of the east.

The Origins of Roman Religion

Many of the gods and goddesses worshipped by the Romans were borrowed from the Greeks, or had their equivalents in Greek mythology. Some of these came by way of the Etruscans or the tribes of Latium. The Diana to whom [the early Roman king] Servius Tullius built the temple on the Aventine Hill was identified with the Greek Artemis, but some of the rites attached to her at Aricia, the centre from which he transferred her worship, went back to an even mistier past. The priest of Diana at Aricia, who was always a runaway slave, held the title of king. He took office by killing his predecessor, and held it for as long as he was able to defeat other runaway slaves in single combat. A fugitive slave could challenge him by breaking off a branch from a particular tree in the sacred grove; so naturally the resident priest kept a close watch. . . .

Occasionally tradition threw up a deity whose antecedents had been forgotten. Such a one was the goddess Furrina. . . . Her festival was regularly observed on 25 July. Unfortunately, by the middle of the first century BC, no one could remember who she was or why she was being celebrated.

The Romans inherited their preoccupation with examining every natural phenomenon for what it might foretell from the Etruscans, who had developed the practice if not into a science, then at least into an art. The Etruscans employed three main kinds of divination, which were said to have been communicated to them by a mysterious lad called Tages, who appeared to them having literally been ploughed up from the earth while it was being tilled:

1. Divining the future from examining the entrails of victims sacrificed at the altar—the liver was of particular significance.
2. Observing and explaining the meaning of lightning and advising on how sinister predictions might be averted.
3. Interpreting any unusual phenomena and taking necessary action.

Many primitive societies practised animism, the belief that natural and physical objects are endowed with mystical properties. The Romans took this cult so far that they could be said to have made it peculiarly their own. They invested trees, springs, caves, lakes, animals, even household furniture with *numina* (singular *numen*, meaning 'divine power' or 'spirit'). Stones could have spirits, too, especially the boundary stones between one person's property and the next. The word for a boundary stone was *terminus*; there was even a great god Terminus, a massive piece of masonry which stood permanently in the temple of Jupiter on the Capitoline Hill, because, it was said, it refused to budge even for Jupiter.

Prayer and Sacrifice

The contractual relationship between mankind and the gods involved each party in giving, and in return receiving, services. The Romans believed that spirits residing in natural and physical objects had the power to control the processes of nature, and that man could influence these processes by symbolic action. The first is a primitive form of religious creed; the second is a type of magic.

The 'services' by which Romans hoped to influence the forces that guided their lives were firmly established in ritual—the ritual of prayer and the ritual of offering. In either case, the exact performance of the rite was essential. One slip, and you had to go back to the beginning and start again. The very multiplicity of deities caused problems, as did the gender of some of them: 'whether you be god or goddess' is a common formula in Roman prayers. The poet Horace (65–8 B.C.) dedicated to Augustus an ode calling for divine assistance to restore the fortunes of Rome, but is clearly in doubt as to whom his appeal should be addressed: 'Upon which of the gods should the people call to revive the failing empire?' (*Odes*, I. 2). He plays safe by starting at the top of the hierarchy: 'To whom will Jupiter assign the task of receiving atonement for our crimes?' He then cites four candidates in turn: Apollo, Venus, Mars, Mercury. . . .

There were few occasions on which a prayer was inappropriate. There was a prayer for the return of stolen property and another for the diversion of some unspecified piece of ill-fortune to someone else. Some prayers were realistic and modest, for example Horace's 'Poet's Prayer', which ends: 'I pray, Apollo, let me be content with what I have, enjoy good health and clarity of mind, and in a dignified old age retain the power of verse'

(*Odes*, I. 31). This is, however, about the nearest any Roman usually got to praying for anything but material blessings.

Prayer was almost invariably accompanied by some form of offering, or sacrifice. This did not necessarily involve the ritual slaughter of an animal, as long as the offering represented life in some form: it could be millet, cakes made from ears of corn which had been picked a month earlier, fruit, cheese, bowls of wine, or pails of milk. Each deity had his or her own preference—a ram for Janus, a heifer for Jupiter. For Mars it was usually a combination of ox, pig, and sheep, but on 15 October it had to be a race-horse. In fact it had to be the winner: the near-side horse of the winning pair in the chariot race that day was immediately taken to the altar and slaughtered. Then its tail was cut off and the blood that dripped from it preserved as a charm. The sex of a chosen animal was also significant: male for gods, female for goddesses. So was its colour. White beasts were offered to deities of the upper world, black to those of the underworld. . . .

The sacrificial routine was elaborate and messy. The head of the victim was sprinkled with wine and bits of sacred cake made from flour and salt. Then its throat was cut and it was disembowelled to ensure there was nothing untoward about its entrails. If there was, it was not only a bad omen, but the whole process had to be repeated with a fresh animal until it came out right. The vital organs were burnt upon the altar and the carcase cut into pieces and eaten on the spot, or else laid aside. Then the priest, wearing something over his face to shut out evil influences from his eyes, would say prayers, speaking under his breath, while a flute was played to drown any ill-omened noise. Any unintentional deviation from the prescribed ritual meant not only a new sacrifice, but an additional one in expiation of the error. The victim in this case was usually a pig. On high occasions, on which a replay of the entire ceremony might be an embarrassment, an expiatory sacrifice was performed as a matter of course on the previous day, in the hope of atoning for any sin of omission or error on the day itself. . . .

Omens

A sibyl was a Greek prophetess. The story goes that one of her kind offered to Tarquinius Superbus [Rome's last king] a collection of prophecies and warnings in the form of nine books at a high price. When he refused, she threw three of them into the fire and offered him the remaining six at the original price of the nine. He refused again; she burned three more and offered him the surviving three, still at the same price. This time he bought them, at what he could have paid for all nine. The Sibylline Books were consulted on the orders of the senate at times of crisis and calamity, in order to learn how the wrath of the gods could be allayed. They were accidentally burned in 83 B.C., and envoys were sent all round the known world to collect a set of similar utterances. Augustus had the new collection put in the temple of Apollo on the Palatine Hill, where it remained until it was finally destroyed in the fifth century A.D.

Disasters were seen by the Romans as manifestations of divine disapproval, and unusual phenomena as portents of catastrophe. In the winter of 218/217 B.C., just before the battle of Trasimene . . . the following portents were said to have been observed:

> In Rome a 6-month-old freeborn infant shouted 'Victory' in the vegetable market; in the cattle market an ox climbed up three flights of stairs on its own and then jumped out of a window in fright when the inhabitants screamed; phantom ships glowed in the sky; the temple of Hope, in the vegetable market, was struck by lightning. In Lanuvium a sacrificial corpse moved and a crow flew down into the temple of Juno and alighted on her sacred couch. In the district of Amiternum, ghostly men in shining garb materialized in many places but did not approach anyone. In Picenum it rained stones. At Caere oracular tablets shrank. In Gaul a wolf stole a sentry's sword from its sheath and ran off with it.

(Livy, History of Rome, XXI. 62)

Reports of phenomena such as these could cause panic among a people for whom superstition was a way of life, especially at times of national uncertainty. The Sibylline Books were promptly consulted, except apparently about the case of the raining stones, which it was felt could be dealt with by an official period of nine days' prayer. Various methods of appeasement emerged for the rest, including the ceremonial purging of the entire city of Rome, sacrifices, gifts to temples of Juno of gold ingots (each weighing 40 lb) and bronze statues, and a series of symbolic feasts at which statues of the gods were laid in reclining positions on couches round a banqueting table. At the end of it all, Livy reports, the Roman people felt considerably relieved.

The awe in which the Sibylline Books were held and the reverence with which their revelations were treated illustrate their significance in the Romans' relationship with their gods. The taking of omens or auspices—the literal meaning of the latter is 'signs from birds'—was a standard procedure before any state activity. . . . An official augur, who was present on such occasions merely as a consultant, marked out and prepared the statutory square measure of ground and then handed over to the state official who was to perform the ritual. He took up his position and observed the flights of any birds he could see, their kind, height, position, speed, direction of flight. If there was any doubt about the interpretation of what the official saw, the augur was called upon to advise. Later, armies took with them a portable auspice-kit, consisting of a cage of sacred chickens, in front of whom bits of cake were placed to see what would happen. It was a bad sign if they refused to eat: good if they ate the cake and let bits of grain fall from their beaks. . . .

There was a distinction between signs that were solicited and those which appeared without invitation. The more startling or unexpected the sign, for instance a sudden flash of lightning or an epileptic fit on the part of a member of an assembly, the more seriously it was taken. It was not unknown for an interested party to throw a feigned fit in order to obstruct proceedings. Lightning which appeared while auspices were being taken was good news: not so when it came unbidden. In 114 B.C. the unthinkable happened and a vestal virgin, [one of Rome's most sacred priestesses] was struck by lightning. A special commission was set up which by dubious means procured the conviction of several other vestals for sexual offences. Hysteria was still not abated, and the senate called for a reading from the Sibylline Books. . . .

Worship in the Home

Two national deities had their place in private worship too: Vesta, goddess of the fire and the hearth, and Janus, god of doorways. Janus, who gave his name to the month of January, is often depicted as having two faces, one looking in each direction. For this there are several interpretations: that it represents opening and closing a door, going in and coming out, or viewing (and thus guarding) both the inside and outside of a house. The door itself was so highly regarded that it required the attention of three more deities: Cardea, goddess of hinges; Limentinus, god of the threshold; and Forculus, who presided over the individual leaf or leaves. Vesta was particularly important to the women of the household, for the hearth was where the food was prepared and cooked, and beside it the meal was eaten. Prayers were said to Vesta every day, and during a meal a portion of food might be thrown into the fire as an offering, and also to seek omens from the way in which it burned.

The particular gods of the household were its *lares* and *penates*. The *lares* (one of them was designated *lar familiaris* or 'family spirit' and was special to that household) were supposed to be the spirits of dead ancestors, and had a cupboard of their own which they inhabited in the form of tiny statuettes. Daily prayers and offerings were made to them, with more elaborate ones on the sacred days of each month—the calends, ides, and nones—and on notable occasions such as a birth, wedding, birthday, a departure or return, or the first word spoken by a son of the house. The *penates* looked after the larder [pantry], its contents and their replenishment, and also had their own cupboard. The statuettes of the *penates* used to be taken out and put on the table at mealtimes, and were sometimes given the names of particular state gods. When the family moved, its *lares* and *penates* went too.

Each household had in addition its *genius*, whose image was a house-snake. *Genius* might be described as a 'spirit of manhood', since it was supposed to give a man the power of generation, and its particular sphere of influence was the marriage-bed. The household *genius* was especially honoured on the birthday of the head of the family.

Births, marriages, and deaths all had their special rituals. Juno Lucina was, as we have seen, the main deity of childbirth, but there were other spirits who watched over the embryo child and its mother from the moment of conception to the birth itself. Immediately after the birth, a sacred meal was offered to Picumnus and Pilumnus, two jolly rustic deities, for whom a made-up bed was kept in some conjugal bedrooms. A positive string of child-development deities watched over the baby's breast-feeding, bones, posture, drinking, eating, and talking, even its accent. On the ninth day after the birth of a boy, the eighth in the case of a girl, the ceremony of purification and naming was enacted, presided over by the goddess Nundina. . . .

While a spirit of some kind watched over a person at most times and on most occasions from conception to death, at the actual moment of death there was none. The religious element in the funeral rites was directed towards a symbolic purification of the survivors. After the burial or cremation, a sow was sacrificed to Ceres to cleanse the house, and any refuse in it was solemnly swept out, while the family was sprinkled with water, and then invited to step over a ceremonial fire. After that, everyone sat down to a feast. Once the corpse was buried—and even in the case of cremation one bone was preserved and put in the ground—its own spirit joined all those other spirits of the dead, which were known collectively as *manes* and required regular worship and appeasement. There were also mischievous spirits of the dead, known as *larvae* or *lemures*, which could, however, be exorcized [cast out] by the master of the house performing an elaborate ritual, involving the spitting out of black beans and the clanking of brass pots. . . .

The Religion of the State

The religion of the Roman state reflected the ways of private worship, while retaining traditions from the period of the kings. Under the nominal direction of the *pontifex maximus*, administrative and ritualistic matters were the responsibility of four colleges, whose members, with one or two exceptions, were appointed or elected from the ranks of politicians and held office for life.

The members of the Pontifical College, the senior body, were the *rex sacrorum, pontifices, flamines*, and the vestal virgins. *Rex sacrorum* (king of religious rites) was an office created under the early republic to maintain the tradition of royal authority over religious matters. Though in later times he still took precedence at religious ceremonies over all other dignitaries including the *pontifex maximus*, it had by then become largely an honorary position.

The sixteen *pontifices* (priests) were the chief administrators and organizers of the religious affairs of the state, and authorities on procedure and matters of the calendar and festivals, and on the designation of particular days on which certain public business could not be conducted.

The *flamines* were priests of particular gods: three for the major gods, Jupiter, Mars, and Quirinus, and twelve for the lesser ones. These specialists had the technical knowledge of the worship of the particular deity to whom, and to whose temple, they were attached, and performed the daily sacrifice to each. The *flamen dialis* (priest of Jupiter) was the most important of them, and on certain occasions he ranked alongside the *pontifex maximus* and the *rex sacrorum*. His life was hedged around with taboos and hazards. [The second-century A.D. Roman writer] Aulus Gellius recorded, while living in Greece, 'those I can remember'. They included the following:

> He may not ride a horse. . . . If a person is brought into the house of the *flamen dialis* in fetters, he must be untied and the bonds pulled up through the open skylight on to the roof and then let down into the street. . . . Only a free man may cut his hair. It is the custom that the *flamen dialis* may not touch or even mention a nanny-goat, uncooked meat, ivy, or beans. . . . He may not go out without his cap of office; it has only recently been decided by the priests that he can take it off indoors. . . . If he loses his wife, he must resign his office. His marriage cannot be ended except by death.
>
> (*Attic Nights*, X. 15)

To perform rituals of worship, Vestal Virgins received years of vigorous training. They held a prestigious position in Roman society.

The six vestal virgins were chosen from ancient patrician families at an early age to serve at the temple of Vesta. They normally served ten years as novices, the next ten performing the duties, and a further ten teaching the novices. They had their own convent near the forum, and their duties included guarding the sacred fire in the temple, performing the rituals of worship, and baking the salt cake which was used at various festivals throughout the year. Punishment for any lapse in ritual or conduct was rigorous: whipping for letting the sacred fire go out; whipping and being walled up underground, with a few provisions, for a breach of the vow of chastity. The prestige of being a vestal virgin, however, was considerable. . . .

The fifteen members of the College of Augurs exercised great learning, and presumably also diplomacy, in the interpretation of omens in public and private life, and acted as consultants in cases of doubt. Each carried a crooked staff, without any knot in it, with which he marked out the square space of ground from which official auspices were observed.

The members of the College of 'Quindecemviri Sacris Faciundis' (Fifteen for Special Religious Duties) were the keepers of the Sibylline Books, which they consulted and interpreted when requested to do so, and ensured that any actions prescribed were properly carried out. They also had responsibility for supervising the worship of any foreign deity which was introduced into the religion of the state from time to time, usually on the recommendation of the Sibylline Books. Such a one was Cybele, the Phrygian goddess of nature, whose presence in Rome in the form of a sacred slab of black meteoric rock was recommended in 204 B.C. after . . . it had rained stones more often than usual. The cult itself, symbolized by noisy processions of attendant eunuch priests and flagellants [worshipers who whipped themselves], was exotic and extreme, in direct contrast to the stately, methodical practices of state religion. . . . The annual public games . . . in honour of Cybele, the 'Great Mother', were held in considerable style from 4 to 10 April, and were preceded by a ceremonial washing and polishing of her stone by members of the college. . . .

The survival of a religious faith depends on a continual renewal and affirmation of its beliefs, and sometimes on adapting its ritual to changes in social conditions and attitudes. . . . To the Romans, the observance of religious rites was a public duty rather than a private impulse. Their beliefs were founded on a variety of unconnected and often inconsistent mythological traditions, many of them derived from Greek rather than Italian models. Without any basic creed to counter, foreign religions made inroads into a society whose class-structure was being blurred and whose constitution was being changed by the increased presence of freed slaves and of incomers from abroad. The brilliance of some of the major foreign cults had considerable attraction for those brought up on homespun deities of the hearth and fields. The first of these to reach Rome was that of Cybele. . . in 204 B.C. The worship of Mithras, the emissary of light who symbolized the fight to disseminate life-giving forces in the face of the powers of darkness and disorder, reached Rome from Persia in the first century AD and had a particular appeal to the army. . . .

The worship of the Egyptian goddess Isis came to Rome in the early years of the first century BC. Its significance is powerfully reflected in the fictional prose narrative *Metamorphoses* (also known as *The Golden Ass*) by Lucius Apuleius (*fl. c.* A.D. 160), who became a priest of Isis and her consort Osiris. The protagonist, also called Lucius, is accidentally turned into an ass; after several adventures and misadventures he appeals for help to Isis, having realized the omnipotence of the 'supreme goddess'. She duly appears to him [and transforms him back into a person]. . . .

The worship of Isis in the Roman empire was just one of the cults known as 'mysteries', which were of Greek origin. The mysteries based on Eleusis, and those of Cybele and Bacchus, were also significant. They all have in common a ceremony of purification of the initiate, a sense of personal relationship with the deity, and an understanding of a life beyond death. . . .

The mysteries were cults whose rituals were known only to initiates, who appear closely to have guarded the secrets of them— as well they might, considering the restrictions on any worship which conflicted with that of the state. What do remain, however, apart from literary allusions, are fascinating glimpses, preserved by nature in the lava from the eruption of Vesuvius in A.D. 79, of the cults of Isis and Bacchus, in the form of wall paintings uncovered at and near Pompeii. . . .

[Not wanting to see the imported Eastern religions overshadow the older state religion, the first emperor] Augustus, as a part of his national morale-boosting campaign, reaffirmed the traditional forms of worship. He restored eighty-two temples in and around Rome, it is claimed all in the space of one year, and in 12 B.C. had himself appointed *pontifex maximus,* a post which thereafter was restricted to emperors. Thus the head of state was once again the head also of religious affairs. He especially promoted the god Apollo, with whom his own family was said to have special affinities, to the status of a major deity, and dedicated a magnificent new temple to him on a site on the Palatine Hill which was his personal property. He did not take the connection between religion and rule so far as to allow himself officially to be regarded as a god in his own lifetime, but he prepared the way to being deified after his death by confirming the divinity of Julius Caesar and dedicating a temple to him. . . .

In about A.D. 30, in the reign of Tiberius, a young Jewish thinker and teacher, son of a carpenter in Nazareth, was executed in Jerusalem under Roman law. His name was Jesus, and he was held to be the Messiah. While his death was hardly noticed by Roman historians, with hindsight it is perhaps not so remarkable that the first adherents to a new and personalized religion, which had its roots and basic teachings in intellectually the most acceptable faith of the times, should have succeeded in spreading its message through the ancient world. This was especially the case among the lower orders, for whom this new faith seemed to offer a bond of unity with one another, and a means of worshipping a single spiritual god by giving honour to a being with whom they could identify.

During the second century A.D. Christians were persecuted for their beliefs largely because these did not allow them to give the statutory reverence to the images of the gods and of the emperor, and because their act of worship [took place in secret, and was therefore suspicions]. . . . To the government, it was civil disobedience: to the Christians themselves it was the suppression of their freedom of worship. [Despite the persecutions, the Christians persevered. Aided by the tolerant emperor Constantine I, in the fourth century A.D. they gained increasing acceptance; and by the end of that century Christianity had become the state religion.]

A Ceremony Honoring the Goddess Isis

Apuleius

Of the many Eastern religions that spread through the Mediterranean world in the late Republic and early Empire, one of the most popular was that of Isis. This fertility and marriage goddess originated in Egypt as the sister and wife of the god Osiris (whom the Romans came to call Sarapis) and the mother of the god Horus (the Roman Harpocrates). The Greeks identified her with Aphrodite (goddess of love). When Isis was imported into Roman society, she was viewed as a kind and compassionate mother figure, sometimes pictured in art holding or nursing her son (which influenced later portrayals of the Virgin Mary and baby Jesus) and her cult became widely popular. The rituals and beliefs of Isis's cult, which were similar to those of the mystery religions, included initiation, baptism, and the promise of eternal salvation. Fortunately, the second-century A.D. Roman writer Apuleius preserved a detailed description of one of Isis's two most important festivals in *The Golden Ass*, the only Roman novel that survives complete (the fanciful story of a young man who is transformed into an ass through black magic and back into a person by the power of the sympathetic goddess). The festival, called the Launching of Isis's Ship, took place annually on March 5 to celebrate the advent of spring and the renewal of life that accompanies it.

The clouds of dark night were dispersed, and a golden sun arose. There and then groups of people filled the entire streets, darting here and there in quite exultant devotion. My personal sense of well-being seemed to be compounded by a general atmosphere of joy, which was so pervasive that I sensed that every kind of domestic beast, and entire households, and the very weather seemed to present a smiling face to the world. For a sunny, windless day had suddenly succeeded the previous day's frost, so that even the birds were enticed by the spring warmth to burst tunefully into sweet harmonies, as with their charming address they soothed the mother of the stars, the parent of the seasons, the mistress of the entire world. Why, even the trees, both those fertile with their produce of fruit, and the barren ones content with the provision of mere shade, expanded under the southerly breezes, and smiled with the budding of their foliage; they whispered sweetly with the gentle motion of their branches. Now that the great din of the storms was stilled, and the waves' angry swell had subsided, the sea quietened and controlled its floods, while the sky dispersed the dark rain-clouds and shone with the cloudless and bright brilliance of its light.

The Sacred Procession

And now the outrunners of the great procession formed up to lead the way, each most handsomely adorned in the garb of his choice. . . .

The special procession in honour of the saviour goddess was being set in motion. Some women, sparkling in white dresses, delighting in their diverse adornments and garlanded with spring flowers, were strewing the ground with blossoms stored in their dresses along the route on which the sacred company was to pass. Others had gleaming mirrors attached to their backs to render homage to the goddess as she drew near them, and others with ivory combs gestured with their arms and twirled their fingers as if adorning and combing their queen's tresses. Others again sprinkled the streets with all manner of perfumes, including the pleasing balsam-scent which they shook out in drops. Besides these there was a numerous crowd of both sexes who sought the favour of the creator of the celestial stars by carrying lamps, torches, tapers and other kinds of artificial light. Behind them came musical instruments, pipes and flutes which sounded forth the sweetest melodies. There followed a delightful choir of specially chosen youths clad in expensive white tunics, who kept hymning a charming song composed to music by a talented poet with the aid of the Muses [goddesses of the fine arts]; the theme incorporated chants leading up to the greater votive prayers to follow. In the procession too were flautists dedicated to the great god Sarapis; the pipes in their hands extended sideways to their right ears, and on them they repeatedly played the tune regularly associated with their temple and its god. There were also several officials loudly insisting that a path be cleared for the sacred procession.

Next, crowds of those initiated into the divine rites came surging along, men and women of every rank and age, gleaming with linen garments spotlessly white. The women had sprayed their hair with perfume, and covered it with diaphanous veils; the men had shaved their heads completely, so that their bald pates shone. With their rattles of bronze, silver, and even gold, they made a shrill, tinkling sound. Accompanying them were the stars of the great world-religion, the priests of the cult who were drawn from the ranks of famed nobility; they wore white linen garments which fitted tightly across their chests and extended to their feet, and they carried striking attributes of most powerful deities. Their leader held out a lamp gleaming with brilliant light; it did not much resemble those lanterns of ours which illumine our banquets at night, but it was a golden, boat-shaped vessel feeding quite a large flame from an opening at its centre. The second priest was similarly garbed; he carried in both hands the altar which they call the 'altar of help', a name specifically bestowed on it by the providential help of the highest goddess. A third priest advanced, bearing a palm-branch, its leaves finely worked in gold; he carried also the staff of Mercury [the Roman messenger god]. A fourth priest exhibited a deformed left hand with palm outstretched, symbolizing justice; since it was impaired by nature and endowed with no guile or cunning, it was thought more suited to represent justice than the right hand. He also carried a small golden vessel rounded like a woman's breast, from which he poured libations of milk. A fifth priest bore a winnowing-fan of gold, fashioned from laurel-twigs, and a sixth carried an amphora.

Immediately behind marched gods who deigned to advance on human feet. Here was Anubis, the awesome go-between of gods above and subterranean dwellers; with face part-black, part-golden, tall and holding his dog's neck high, he carried a herald's staff in his left hand, and brandished a green palm-branch in his right. Hard on his heels followed a cow rearing upright, the fertile representation of the goddess who is mother of all; a member of the priesthood held it resting on his shoulders, and he bore it with a flourish and with proud gait. Another carried the box containing the mysteries [the goddess's sacred objects] and concealing deep within it the hidden objects of that august religion. Yet another priest bore in exultant arms the venerable image of the supreme deity. It was not in the shape of a farm-animal or bird or wild beast or the human form itself, but in its ingenious originality it inspired veneration by its very strangeness, for it expressed in a manner beyond description the higher religious faith which has to be cloaked in boundless silence. Fashioned from gleaming gold, this was a small vase skilfully hollowed out on a perfectly rounded base, with remarkable Egyptian figures fashioned on its outer surface; it had not a high neck, but it projected into a long spout extending into a beak. On its other side a handle was set well back in a broad curve, and above it was an asp coiled in a knot, the striped swelling of its scaly neck rearing high. . . .

Launching the Ship

I then took my place in the sacred procession and walked along, keeping close attendance on the sacred shrine. I was recognized, indeed I was the cynosure [center of attention] of all eyes; the whole community singled me out with pointing fingers and nods, and gossiped about me: 'Today the venerable power of the almighty goddess has restored him to the ranks of men. How happy, how blessed three times over he is! Doubtless through the purity and faith of his former life he has deserved such sovereign protection from heaven, and in consequence he had been in a manner reborn, and has at once pledged himself to the service of her cult.'

Meanwhile amid the din of joyous prayers we edged our way slowly forward and drew near to the sea-shore, at that very place where as Lucius-turned-ass I had bivouacked [camped out] the previous day. There the gods' statues were duly set in place, and the chief priest named and consecrated to the goddess a ship which had been built with splendid craftsmanship, and which was adorned on all its timbers with wonderful Egyptian pictures. Holding a flaming torch, he first pronounced most solemn prayers from his chaste lips, and then with an egg and sulphur he performed over it an elaborate ceremony of purification. The bright sail of this blessed craft carried upon it woven letters in gold, bearing those same petitions for trouble-free sailing on its first journeys. The mast was of rounded pine, gloriously tall and easily recognized with its striking masthead. The stern was curved in the shape of a goose, and gleamed with its covering of gold leaf. In fact the whole ship shone, polished as it was in clear citrus-wood.

Then the entire population, devotees and uninitiated alike, vied in piling the ship high with baskets laden with spices and similar offerings, and they poured on the waves libations of meal soaked in milk. Eventually the ship, filled with generous gifts and propitious offerings, was loosed from its anchor-ropes and launched on the sea before a friendly, specially appointed breeze. Once its progress had caused it to fade from our sight, the bearers of the sacred objects took up again those which each had brought, and they made their eager way back to the temple, following in tidy order the same detail of procession as before.

Once we reached the temple itself, the chief priest, those who carried the gods' images, and those previously initiated into the august inner sanctuary were admitted into the chamber of the goddess, where they duly set in place the living statues. Then one of the company, whom they all termed the scribe, stood before the entrance and summoned an assembly of the *pastophori*; this is the name of the sacred college [organization of priests]. There from a high dais [speaker's platform] he first recited from a book formulaic prayers for the prosperity of the great emperor, the senate, the knights, and the entire Roman people; then for sea-travellers and for ships journeying within the bounds of our imperial world. Next he announced in the Greek language and according to Greek ritual the ceremony of the launching of the ships. The applause of the people that followed showed that this speech was well received by all. Then the folk, ecstatic with joy, brought up boughs, branches and garlands, and having kissed the feet of the goddess (her statue, wrought from silver, was attached to the temple-steps), they departed to their homes. But my enthusiasm did not permit me to separate myself by more than a nail's breadth from that spot, and I gazed intently on the image of the goddess as I pondered my earlier misfortunes.

Roman Wedding Celebrations

Harold W. Johnston

Roman marriage was an ancient and respected social institution and also crucial because it made one's children legitimate in the eyes of the law and the community. There were different forms of the marriage union, the earliest known as *confarreatio*. It consisted of the bride passing from her father's home (and his authority) into the house and protection/control (*manus*) of her new husband. If she did not originally belong to his clan (*gens*), she entered it on marrying him. This kind of marriage was at first engaged in mainly by aristocrats and wealthy people and the ceremony occurred in the presence of Rome's chief priest (*pontifex maximus*), making it sacred. The early plebeians (common people) had marriages, too, which were of two types. The oldest was called *usus*. It consisted of the man and woman living together continuously, perhaps for some customary period of time. The other early type of plebeian marriage was *coemptio*, a fictitious "sale" or "freeing" in which a father transferred his daughter and all of her rights to her new husband. Over the centuries, Roman marriage customs changed considerably. Marriage between nobles and commoners, for instance, became legal and eventually fairly common. At the same time, marriages involving *manus* became increasingly less common. By the first century B.C., *usus* was no longer in use, while *confarreatio* and *coemptio* were fairly rare. *Justae nuptiae*, what might be described as a more "regular" kind of marriage (from a modern viewpoint), had become and thereafter remained the norm.

Each of the early forms of marriage had distinct wedding ceremonies, which are described in this fascinating tract by former Indiana University scholar Harold W. Johnston. But as he points out, these grew increasingly similar over time. From the first century B.C. on, the typical wedding celebration combined numerous elements from all of the earlier, traditional versions.

Harold W. Johnston, *The Private Life of the Romans*. New York: Scott, Foresman and Company, 1903.

In connection with the marriage ceremonies it must be remembered that only the consent [of the man and woman to get married] was necessary, with the act expressing the consent, and that all other forms and ceremonies were nonessential and variable. Something depended upon the particular form used, but more upon the wealth and social position of the families interested. It is probable that most weddings were a good deal simpler than those described by our chief authorities [i.e., the ancient writers whose works have survived]. The house of the bride's father, where the ceremony was performed, was decked with flowers, boughs of trees, bands of wool, and tapestries. The guests arrived before the hour of sunrise, but even then the omens had been already taken. . . .

After the omens had been pronounced favorable, the bride and groom appeared in the atrium, the public room of the house, and the wedding began. This consisted of two parts:

(1) The ceremony proper, varying according to the form used (*confarreatio, coemptio,* or *usus*), the essential part being the consent before witnesses.

(2) The festivities, including the feast at the bride's home, the taking of the bride with a show of force from her mother's arms, the escorting of the bride to her new home (the essential part), and her reception there.

Gaius and Gaia

The confarreate ceremony began [when] the bride and groom were brought together by the *pronuba*, a matron but once married and living with her husband in undisturbed wedlock. They joined hands in the presence of ten witnesses. . . . These are shown on an ancient sarcophagus found at Naples. Then followed the words of consent spoken by the bride: *Quando tu Gaius, ego Gaia.* The words mean, "When (and where) you are Gaius, then (and there) I am Gaia," i.e., "I am bone of your bone, flesh of your flesh." The formula was unchanged, no matter what the names of the bride and groom, and goes back to a time when *Gaius* was a *nomen* [clan name], not a *praenomen* [personal name]. It implied that the bride was actually entering the *gens* of the groom, and was probably chosen for the lucky meaning of the names *Gaius* and *Gaia.* . . . The bride and groom then took their places side by side at the left of the altar and facing it, sitting on stools covered with the pelt of the sheep slain for the sacrifice.

A bloodless offering was made to Jupiter by the *Pontifex Maximus* and the *Flamen Dialis,* consisting of the cake of spelt (*farreum libum*) from which the ceremony got the name *confarreatio.* Then the cake was eaten by the bride and groom. With the offering to Jupiter a prayer was recited by the Flamen [priest] to Juno as the goddess of marriage, and to Tellus, Picumnus, and Pilumnus, deities of the country and its fruits. The utensils necessary for the offering were carried in a covered basket (*cumera*) by a boy called *camillus,* whose parents must both be living at the time. . . . Then followed the congratulations, the guests using the word *feliciter* ["with luck and happiness"].

The *coemptio* began with the fictitious sale, carried out in the presence of no fewer than five witnesses. The purchase money, represented by a single coin, was laid in the scales. . . . The scales, scaleholder, coin, and witnesses were all necessary for this kind of marriage. Then followed the . . . words of consent, borrowed, as has been said, from the confarreate ceremony. . . .

A prayer was then recited and sometimes, perhaps, a sacrifice was offered, after which came the congratulations, as in the other and more elaborate ceremony.

The third form, that is, the ceremonies preliminary to *usus,* probably admitted of more variation than either of the others, but no description has come down to us. We may be sure that the hands were clasped, the words of consent spoken, and congratulations offered, but we know of no special customs or usages. It was almost inevitable that the three forms should become more or less alike in the course of time, though the cake of spelt could not be borrowed from the confarreate ceremony by either of the others, or the scales and their holder from the ceremony of *coemptio.*

The Feast and Procession

After the conclusion of the ceremony came the wedding feast (*cena nuptialis*), lasting in early times until evening. There can be no doubt that this was regularly given at the house of the bride's father and that the few cases when, as we know, it was given at the groom's house were exceptional and due to special circumstances which might cause a similar change today. The feast seems to have concluded with the distribution among the guests of pieces of the wedding cake (*mustaceum*). There came to be so much extravagance at these feasts . . . that under Augustus it was proposed to limit their cost by law to one thousand sesterces. . . . His efforts to limit such expenditures were, however, fruitless.

After the wedding feast the bride was formally taken to her husband's house. This ceremony was called *deductio*, and, since it was essential to the validity of the marriage, it was never omitted. It was a public function, that is, anyone might join the procession and take part in the merriment that distinguished it; we are told that persons of rank did not scruple to wait in the street to see a bride. As evening approached, the procession was formed before the bride's house with torch-bearers and flute-players at its head. When all was ready, the marriage hymn (*hymenaeus*) was sung and the groom took the bride with a show of force from the arms of her mother. The Romans saw in this custom a reminiscence of the rape of the Sabines, but it probably goes far back beyond the founding of Rome to the custom of marriage by capture that prevailed among many peoples. The bride then took her place in the procession. She was attended by three boys. Two of these walked beside her, each holding one of her hands, while the other carried before her the wedding torch of white thorn (*spina alba*). Behind the bride were carried the distaff and spindle, emblems of domestic life. The *camillus* . . . also walked in the procession.

During the march were sung the *versus Fescennini*, abounding in coarse jests and personalities. [These were probably somewhat like modern dirty limericks, only sung rather than spoken.] The crowd also shouted the ancient marriage cry, the significance of which the Romans themselves did not understand. We find it in at least five forms, all variations of Talassius or Talassio, the name, probably, of a Sabine divinity, whose functions, however, are unknown. [The first-century B.C. Roman historian] Livy derives it from the supposed name of a senator in the time of Romulus. On the way the bride, by dropping one of three coins which she carried, made an offering to the *Lares Compitales*, the gods of the crossroads. Of the other two she gave one to the groom as an emblem of the dowry she brought him, and one to the *Lares* of his house. The groom meanwhile scattered nuts through the crowd. This is explained by [the poet] Catullus that the groom had become a man and had put away childish things, but the nuts were rather a symbol of fruitfulness. The custom survives in the throwing of rice in modern times.

The Threshold and Lucky Torch

When the procession reached the groom's house, the bride wound the door posts with bands of wool, probably a symbol of her own work as mistress of the household, and anointed the door with oil and fat, emblems of plenty. She was then lifted carefully over the threshold, in order, some say, to avoid the chance of so bad an omen as a slip of the foot on entering the house for the first time. Others, however, see in the custom another survival of marriage by capture. She then pronounced again the words of consent: *Ubi tu Gaius, ego Gaia*, and the doors were closed against the general crowd; only the invited guests entered with the newly-married pair.

The husband met his wife in the atrium and offered her fire and water in token of the life they were to live together and of her part in the home. Upon the hearth was ready the wood for a fire; this the bride kindled with the marriage torch, which had been carried before her. The torch was afterwards thrown among the guests to be scrambled for as a lucky possession. A prayer was then recited by the bride and she was placed by the *pronuba* on the *lectus genialis* [bridal couch], which always stood in the atrium on the wedding night. Here it afterwards remained as a piece of ornamental furniture only. On the next day there was given in the new home the second wedding feast to the friends and relatives, and at this feast the bride made her first offering to the gods as a *matrona* [married woman]. A series of feasts followed, given in honor of the newly-wedded pair by those in whose social circles they moved.

A Song for the God of Weddings

Catullus

Gaius Valerius Catullus (ca.84–ca.54 B.C.) was a distinguished and popular Roman poet who composed several poems in the style of the songs people sang during traditional wedding processions. This one, written for the wedding of two acquaintances—Manlius and Junia—praises the god of weddings, Hymen Hymenaeus, and asks that the deity bless the marriage, bride, and groom. Hymen was thought to be the son of Apollo (god of prophecy) and Urania, one of the Muses (goddesses of the arts); hence the song begins with a reference to Helicon, a mountain in Greece sacred to Apollo and the Muses.

O you dweller on the hill
Of Helicon, Urania's breed,
You who kidnap tender bride
For groom, O Hymeneal Hymen,
O Hymen Hymeneal,   5

Wreathe your temples with the flower
Of sweet-smelling marjoram;
Take the flame-hued veil and gladly
Hither come, on snow-white foot
Wearing yellow sandal.   10

Excited by the merry day,
With ringing tenor voice join in
The wedding chorus, beat the ground
With dancing feet and in your hand
Shake the torch of pinewood [the "lucky" torch].   15

For Junia, as beautiful
As Idalium's mistress
Venus coming to the Phrygian
Judge [a reference to the love goddess hoping to receive

Catullus, *The Poems of Catullus*, edited and translated by Guy Lee. New York: Oxford University Press, 1990. Copyright © 1990 by Guy Lee. Reproduced by permission of the publisher.

an award for beauty from Paris, prince of Troy], is
  wedding Manlius,
Good maiden with good omen,   20

Like an Asian myrtle-bush
Shining bright with flowering twigs,
Which Hamadryad Goddesses
Nourish with the drops of dew
As their own plaything. . . .   25

Is any God more to be sought
After by belovèd lovers?
Which Heavenly One will humans sooner
Worship, O Hymeneal Hymen,
O Hymen Hymeneal?   50

The trembling parent prays to you
For his children, virgins loose
The girdle of their dress for you,
And for you the scared new husband
Listens with keen ear.   55

Into the hands of a rough youth
From the bosom of her mother
You commit a bride in tender
Bloom, O Hymeneal Hymen,
O Hymen Hymeneal.   60

Without you Venus can gain
No advantage good repute
Would approve of, but she can
With your favour. Who would dare
Compare with this God?   65

Without you no house can have
Free-born children and no parent
Depend on offspring, but they can
With your favour. Who would dare
Compare with this God?   70

Any land without your rites
Cannot produce guardians
Of its borders, but it can
With your favour. Who would dare

Compare with this God?. . .   75

Please come out, new bride, if now
You are ready, and listen to
Our words. Do you see? The torches
Toss their golden hair about.   95
Please come out, new bride.

Your husband is not light, not tied
To some bad adulteress,
Nor pursuing shameful scandal
Will he wish to sleep apart   100
From your tender nipples,

But, just as the limber vine
Enfolds trees planted beside it,
He will be enfolded in
Your embrace. But day goes by;   105
Please come out, new bride. . . .

Raise the torches high, O boys.
I see the flame-hued veil approach. [The bride's traditional
    wedding dress featured an orange-yellow veil.]   115
Come now, sing together in tune
'O Hymen Hymeneal O,
O Hymen Hymeneal.'

Let the ribald Fescennine
Jesting [singing of off-color verses] not be silent longer   120
Nor boy concubine refuse
Nuts to the children when he hears
Of master's love abandoned. [During the procession, boys
    scattered nuts among the crowd.]

Give the children nuts, you idle
Concubine. For long enough   125
You have played with nuts, but now
It's time to serve Talassius [an ancient Italian god retained
    in the ceremony out of tradition].
Concubine, give nuts. . . .

Here is home for you, your man's
(Look how powerful and blest!) [The procession reaches
    the groom's house.]   150

Which you must allow to serve you
(O Hymen Hymeneal O,
O Hymen Hymeneal)

Till white-haired old-womanhood
With ever nodding head agrees   155
With everyone on everything.
O Hymen Hymeneal O,
O Hymen Hymeneal.

Lift your little golden feet
With good omen over the   160
Threshold, past the polished door. [The groom carries the
    bride over the threshold.]
O Hymen Hymeneal O,
O Hymen Hymeneal.

Look inside, how lying there
Your man on the Tyrian couch [the traditional bridal
    couch]   165
Is totally intent on you.
O Hymen Hymeneal O,
O Hymen Hymeneal.

For him no less than for you
In his inner self there burns   170
A fire, but more inwardly.
O Hymen Hymeneal O,
O Hymen Hymeneal. . . .

And now, bridegroom, you may come.
Your wife is in the bridal chamber,   185
Her face shining like a floret,
Like the white parthenium
Or the yellow poppy.

But, so help me Heaven-Dwellers,
Bridegroom, you are none the less   190
Beautiful. Venus has not
Forgotten you. But day goes by;
Come on, do not linger.

No, you have not lingered long.
Now you're coming. May good Venus   195

Help you, as it's obvious
You desire what you desire
And aren't hiding good love. . . .

Play as you please and very soon
Produce children. It's not right   205
That so old a name should lack
Children, but from the same stock
It should ever sire them. . . .

May he [the first male child] look like Manlius
His father, recognizable   215
By those he meets not in the know
And by his features demonstrate
His mother's chastity. . . .

Close the doors, unmarried girls.
We have played enough. But you,   225
Good wedded couple, live well and
Exercise your lusty youth
In its constant duty.

Building Rome's Mighty Network of Roads

Lionel Casson

Here, from his modern classic, *Travel in the Ancient World,* the noted classical historian Lionel Casson describes one of Roman society's greatest achievements—its system of roads. As Casson explains, these highways connected the capital city of Rome with towns across the vast Empire, allowing rapid transport of armies, as well as facilitating widespread trade, civilian travel, and the spread of Roman social values. Much of the discussion is devoted to the methods Roman engineers and workers used to lay out and construct these roads.

The web of roads that Rome spun the length and breadth of the territory she administered was not only a magnificent achievement, but one of profound significance. It enabled her rulers to establish and maintain the most durable empire in European history; it set the lines along which traders, priests, and soldiers would carry the seeds of change in western civilization; it determined where many of the great urban centres of Europe were to be. Only a rich and powerful state whose authority stretched unchallenged far and wide could have carried out the task, could have built so many thousands of miles of highway, maintained them more or less in good order, fitted them with the appropriate facilities, and given them the essential police protection. When the Roman Empire broke up into a number of independent states, its great road system broke up with it, and, since no nation in the Middle Ages had the necessary organization or money, the fragments gradually degenerated. . . .

The Romans learned the art of roadbuilding from excellent teachers, the Etruscans. This mysterious people, who settled in

Lionel Casson, *Travel in the Ancient World*. Baltimore, MD: Johns Hopkins University Press, 1994. Copyright © 1974 by George Allen & Unwin, Ltd. Reproduced by permission.

what is today Tuscany in the ninth century B.C. and flourished there for half a millennium, has left striking witnesses to their ability as engineers, particularly hydraulic engineers. They taught Rome how to make sewers, aqueducts, bridges, and—more to our present point—properly drained roads. The Etruscans never went beyond well-graded, drained, and carefully surfaced dirt roads. The Romans went one key step further: they added paving. It had long been known, for the Near East had used it for centuries for short distances in special areas. Rome used it for mile upon mile of her major highways.

The first of the great Roman thoroughfares was the Via Appia, the *regina viarum* 'queen of roads', begun in 312 B.C. under Appius Claudius, commissioner of public works for that year. It went to Capua, and then later was carried on to Brindisi, the gateway for travel to the east. A century later two highways leading to the north end of the peninsula were laid down. The Via Flaminia, named after Gaius Flaminius, public works commissioner in 220 B.C., the year construction was started, ran from Rome to Fano on the Adriatic coast, snaking across the Apennines so ingeniously that there were few times in the year when snow closed the passes; some decades later the consul Marcus Aemilius Lepidus added the Via Aemilia, which carried the Flaminia on to Piacenza (it was eventually extended to Milan). The second, the Via Aurelia, which was begun in 144 B.C. or even earlier, took traffic from Rome along the west coast, reaching, with various prolongations, as far as Genoa.

Thus, by the end of the second century B.C., the Italian boot had a set of first-class highways traversing its entire length. The next step was to extend these further, as Rome acquired territories outside of Italy, to permit an uninterrupted flow of soldiers and dispatches from the capital to all points in the Roman sphere of authority. These splendid thoroughfares, we must remember, though used by traders and travellers in plentiful numbers, were built primarily by and for the army. . . .

By the first century A.D., the Mediterranean was girdled along its various coasts by a nearly continuous ring road. Trunk roads and branches radiated from it deep into Europe and Asia, somewhat less deeply into North Africa. In each of Rome's provinces two or three cities came to serve as nodal points for the road web within it. Most have continued to serve, first as road and then as rail centres, and along their approaches Roman paving can often be found under the asphalt or the railway ties. . . .

Initial Planning and Layout

'The roads were carried straight across the countryside without deviation, were paved with hewn stones and bolstered underneath with masses of tight-packed sand; hollows were filled in, torrents or ravines that cut across the route were bridged; the sides were kept parallel and on the same level—all in all, the work presented a vision of smoothness and beauty.' So wrote [the first-century A.D. biographer] Plutarch, describing the construction programme carried out by Gaius Gracchus between 123 and 121 B.C. Plutarch's language is fulsome, but he does not exaggerate: he is describing main highways, and by and large this is the way they were built. The hallmark of a Roman road is the directness of its course. Over the flat it runs like an arrow shot, and even where the terrain is not perfectly level, as in Britain, a stretch can go twenty or thirty miles with only a half-mile deviation. When driving in Europe today you often can tell you are going over what was once a Roman thoroughfare by the way it rolls on and on without a curve.

Rome's prime concern was to have through routes that were usable at all times of year and in all kinds of weather. In other words, they had to be laid on a firm foundation, to be properly drained, and, where traffic was heavy, to be surfaced with a durable paving. This was a tall order for Roman engineers who disposed of limited manpower—the work on main thoroughfares was done by the army which often could not spare troops for the time-consuming job of building roads—and the simplest of tools: pick, hammer, mattock, spade. Rock obstructions had to be painfully picked away, earth obstructions spaded away, and the chips from the one and dirt from the other carried off in baskets, since that superbly useful instrument, the wheelbarrow, though long used by the Chinese, did not reach Europe until the Middle Ages. The feats Rome's road builders were able to perform with this meagre equipment are impressive. There is a point along the coast at Terracina where a huge slice of rock measuring 126 feet from top to bottom was removed from a sheer cliff in order to squeeze the Via Appia in between the cliff and the sea; we know this because the construction gang carved numbers in the rock, starting at the top, to record how many feet they chopped off, and the road ran along at the level of the CXXVI mark. The modern road laid over the Via Flaminia still passes through a forty-yard tunnel that was hacked out in A.D. 77, and there are other tunnels extant (though no longer in use) that measure up to 1,000 yards in length. But the Romans went in for such works only when absolutely unavoidable. Their standard procedure was to take advantage of the terrain rather than fight it, and they did this with great skill.

When building over plains, as in the Po Valley [in northern Italy], they laid their roads straight across, sometimes raised slightly above the level of the land. This not only helped drainage but, in regions that saw snow, enabled the road to stand out even after a heavy fall. In rolling or hilly terrain, rather than putting roads on the floor of the valleys, they favoured running them along the sides, even though this made for curves and added length. At times a modern highway will proceed straight over a valley floor, while its Roman predecessor will be high above, following the twists and turns of the slopes. The point was to avoid laying a bed on marshy or even just damp soil, to avoid the problem of spring floods, and to cross streams high in their course, where they are easy to ford, rather than at their full width where they would have to be bridged. Moreover we must always remember that these roads were built first and foremost for the army, and a slope along one side of a road protected marching troops from attack in that direction. To the Roman planners, extra curves were little enough to pay for these many advantages.

Having determined where a road was to go, the engineers then surveyed its track, a procedure that often taxed their primitive instruments. Roads were laid in segments, and frequently, because of imprecise surveying or imprecise determination of gradients, segments meet each other unevenly or vary in level. Their next step was to make a careful study of the terrain and the soil to see what kind of road-bed they would put down. . . .

Building the Roads

A major road had to have an all-weather surface. Where traffic was light, as in the provinces, the engineers made do with a

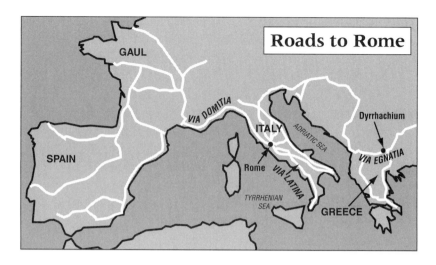

gravel surface. . . . Where traffic was heavy, as along the Via Appia or Flaminia or any of the great highways that fanned out from Rome, they laid a first-quality road, a *via silice strata* 'road paved with silex', i.e. with polygonal paving stones of durable igneous rock, such as basalt (silex), granite, or porphyry. The stones were massive, not uncommonly measuring a foot and a half across and eight inches deep and sometimes much bigger, and were fitted together as cunningly as a jigsaw puzzle to form an absolutely smooth surface. Since igneous rock can be quarried to break off in polygonal chunks, one simple way of getting perfect joints was to put stones together on the road-bed just as they had come out of the quarry; presumably contiguous pieces were marked in the quarries and shipped in a batch. The key problem was to prepare a bed that would not allow any of the stones to sink and form depressions. These were fatal since, over and above the jolts they gave to the passing traffic, they held rainwater which would eventually seep through and undermine the road. As a Roman poet, who had watched the building of a road through soft sandy terrain west of Naples, put it, the engineers had 'to prepare the underbody for a pavement in such a way that the ground would not give, that the foundation would not prove treacherous, that the bed would not prove unstable when the paving blocks pressed down on it [sc. under the weight of traffic]'. Sometimes a road went over land so firm that there was no need whatsoever of a bed and all the gangs had to do was level a track and place the paving stones right on the ground; there is a beautifully preserved stretch of the road that ran from Antioch to Chalcis in Syria laid this way. Where the ground was not that resistant, the gangs trenched until they came to a firm enough layer. Into the trench they set the bed, usually of more or less naturally rounded stones in a mass of clay or clayey earth; the thickness of the bed depended entirely on how deep the trench had to go. When a raised road was called for, as often happened, the bed was built up until it overtopped the ground level to the desired height. The one thing Rome's engineers were finicky about was that the earth or clay used as binder come from elsewhere, not from any trenching done for the road. The sides of the embankments were prevented from being washed away by the addition of terrace walls of either fieldstone or, where a more decorative effect was sought, of squared stone. . . .

Once the bed was ready, the masons set about fitting the paving blocks. These were laid so as to leave the road with a pronounced crown, i.e. higher in the middle than at the sides, in order to shed rainwater. In roads running along slopes the same purpose was achieved by tilting the whole surface toward the lower side. Lastly—or at least on the great thoroughfares—a raised stone border was put along each side, and outside the border an unpaved track, some two feet or so wide, was levelled for pedestrians and pack-animals. At intervals high stones were set along the sides to help a traveller mount a horse—most welcome in an age that did not use stirrups or climb into a high-wheeled carriage. And all highways, whether fitted with border and paths or not, had channels (*fossae*) along one side or both to carry off rainwater. . . .

Curators and Milestones

The government's set-up for administering the road system was calculated to favour Italy at the expense of the provinces. In Italy each highway had its own *curator* or commissioner, charged with keeping it in repair and adequately policed. In the provinces the governor had the responsibility for roads along with everything else, and he simply passed along orders to the local communities: they were to keep the army-built highways in repair and to construct from scratch whatever additional roads were needed. How well or how quickly the orders were executed is another matter: communities were often too hard pressed by taxes and the upkeep of other services to do much about roads.

The last step in building a road was to put up *miliaria* 'milestones'. These were placed every Roman mile (1,000 five-foot paces, hence some ninety-five yards shorter than our mile). In Italy each was inscribed with a figure giving the distance from Rome or from the city where the road started. In the provinces they showed sometimes the distance between towns, sometimes from the roadhead—e.g. roads fanning out from Lyons would carry the number of miles from that city. Occasionally they gave even more information, the distance from either end of the road or from three or four principal points along the road. In Rome itself, at one end of the Forum stood the *miliarium aureum*, the 'golden milestone', which, in letters of gilt, indicated the mileage from Rome along the trunk roads to key points in the empire. Road centres in the provinces had their local equivalent. To the voyager, plodding along on foot or in a slow-moving cart and wondering how long he had to go to get a meal or bed or change of animals, milestones were a godsend, so much so that many a settlement took its name from the stone it was nearest. Some have kept such names right up to the present day.

Horace's Journey on the Appian Way

Horace

In about the year 38 B.C., the famous Roman poet Horace (Quintus Horatius Flaccus, 65–8 B.C.) and some friends made a journey on the Appian Way (or Via Appia), the great road that ran from Rome to the port of Brundisium, on Italy's Adriatic coast, a distance of some 370 miles. This excerpt from Horace's *Satires,* translated by scholars Raymond Chevallier and N.H. Field, tells about the trip. It had a few high points, including fine food and fellowship at a friend's villa; but the narrative reveals that large portions of the journey were uncomfortable, which was typical of long walking tours in ancient times.

When I left mighty Rome, I found bed and board in a modest inn at Aricia [a town about sixteen miles from Rome]. My companion was the rhetorician [speech teacher or orator] Heliodorus, far and away the most learned of the Greeks. Next we reached the Forum of Appius, swarming with sailors and knavish tavern-keepers [the Forum of Appius was a town located about twenty-seven miles from Aricia. From Appius, travelers took a ferry boat across some marshes to reach the next stretch of road.] We felt lazy enough to cut this stretch in two, whereas travellers who gird up their loins take it in one go: the Appian Way is less tiring to those who are not in a hurry. There, by reason of the water, which was frightful, my stomach and I were on hostile terms and I waited with some impatience for my companions, who were dining.

Already the shadows of night were beginning to creep over the earth and stars were pinpointing the heavens. Then slaves bellowed at boatmen and boatmen at slaves: 'Heave to, here', 'You've got three hundred in'! 'Stop! that's enough.' After the fares had been collected and the mule harnessed, a whole hour

Horace, "Appendix 1," *Roman Roads*, edited by Raymond Chevallier, translated by N.H. Field. Berkeley: University of California Press, 1976. Copyright © 1976 by B.T. Batsford, Ltd. Reproduced by permission.

went by. The cursed mosquitoes, the frogs of the marshland drove off sleep. Whereupon, after their fill of poor wine, a boatman and a passenger vied in singing of the girl each of them had left behind. At length, the weary passenger fell asleep and the lazy boatman unharnessed his mule and let it out to graze, tying its leading rein to a stone. Then he too started to snore away on his back. And it was already daylight when we found that the boat was not yet under way. So one of us, hot-headed fellow, jumped ashore and, with a stick cut from a willow, belaboured head and back of both mule and boatman. At last, upon the fourth hour, no earlier, we came ashore. We washed face and hands in thy waters, O Feronia [an ancient Italian goddess who had a spring dedicated to her at the point where the ferry ride ended]! Then, after, having had breakfast, we struggled along for three miles to reach the foot of [the town of Terracina], perched on its white rocks gleaming from afar.

Here the gallant Maecenas and Cocceius were to meet us, both sent as envoys to deal with important matters and both accustomed to bringing together divided friends. Here, too, I made use of a black ointment on my sore eyes. Meantime up came Maecenas and Cocceius, together with Fonteius Capito, a man of matchless perfection, so that Antony can have no closer friend. We were not sorry to leave Fundi [a town lying about thirteen miles beyond Terracina] and its praetor Aufidius Luscus, laughing at the knick-knacks with which that old clerk bedecked himself in his crazy vanity, laughing too at his bordered robe and his broad stripe and his pan of charcoal. Then, weary indeed, we made a long halt in the town of the Mamurrae [residents of the town of Formiae, about thirteen miles from Fundi], where Murena [a friend] provided us with lodging and Capito with board.

Fires, Rain, and Mud

Dawn the next day was most delightful: for at Sinuessa [seventeen miles from Formiae] we were joined by Plotius, Varius and Virgil. Earth has never borne purer souls, there is no man more attached to them than I. Oh! the embraces and the joy! So long as I have my senses, nothing will compare for me to the delight of friendship.

The little post-house close to the Campanian bridge [ten miles beyond Sinuessa] offered us the shelter of its roof, while the state purveyors dutifully provided wood and salt. Next, at the appointed time, our mules laid aside their panniers at Capua. Maecenas went off for exercise, while Virgil and I retired to sleep, for sport is the enemy of weary eyes and sore stomachs.

Our next stop was at the richly furnished villa of Cocceius, situated above the inns of Caudium. . . . A merry company did we make over that meal. Thence we made our way [for a distance of eleven miles] straight to Beneventum, where, in his eagerness to please, our host, was nearly burned up while turning some lean thrushes over the fire. For Vulcan [Roman god of the forge] slipped out and the wandering flame spread through the old kitchen, rising to lick the very roof. Then you would have seen the starving guests and the trembling slaves grabbing the meal, and afterwards doing their best to put out the blaze.

Thenceforward Apulia was beginning to reveal its mountains, which I know so well, scorched by the Altino [a strong local wind] and over which we would never have been able to scramble, had we not found a welcome at a country house in the neighbourhood of Trivicum [about twenty-five miles from Beneventum], not without smoke that drew tears, for in the hearth were burning damp branches, leaves and all. There, in my complete stupidity, I waited until the middle of the night for a lying wench; however, sleep overcame me, impassioned as I still was; and, while I lay on my back, lustful dreams soiled me.

From that point we were taken 24 miles in Gallic carriages, to halt in a small town whose name cannot be put into verse, though it is easy enough to give some clues: the commonest of things, water, is sold there, but the local bread is quite magnificent, so much so that the wise traveller takes a quantity with him as he goes on his way, for at Carnusium the bread is as hard as stone, while there is not a jugful of water to be had in this town founded in bygone days by brave Diomedes [a mythical hero of the Trojan War who was said to have established several towns in Italy]. Here Varius sorrowfully took leave of his weeping friends.

Next we came to Rubi, very weary indeed, for we had gone a very long stage, with conditions made worse furthermore by the rain. The following day, the weather improved, but the track was even viler [i.e., the road was choked with mud] until we reached the walls of the little fishing-port of Barium. Then [the town of] Gnatnia . . . gave us occasion to laugh and make pleasantry: for there people would have it that incense placed on the temple threshold melts without the need of fire. [Those who are gullible] may believe it; I do not, for I have learnt that the gods spend their time eternally at repose and that, if there are extraordinary phenomena produced by nature, it is not they who, to relieve their boredom, send these things down from their heavenly abode on high.

Brundisium is the end of this long tale and this long journey.

Leisure Time: Large and Small-Scale Games

CHAPTER

3

Chapter Preface

The Roman poet and humorist Martial wrote in one of his epigrams: "Alas, what a crime! You were cheated of your youth, Scorpus. . . . Too soon have you harnessed the dark horses of death. Why did the finish line of the race, which you time and again hastened to cross . . . now become the finish of your life?" When these words were written, Flavius Scorpus, a hugely popular charioteer who had won more than two thousand races, had died at the tender age of twenty-six in a crash on the racetrack.

That other Roman writers noted and hundreds of thousands of fans mourned Scorpus's passing is understandable. The Romans cherished their leisure hours and whenever possible filled them with enjoyable activities. But above all they adored chariot races, especially those held in the Circus Maximus, Rome's largest and most prestigious racetrack. Begun in the early Republic and expanded and improved over the centuries, the so-called Great Circus was, by the early second century A.D., so large and splendid that it was easily one of the marvels of the world.

Those charioteers like Scorpus, who raced in the Circus Maximus and other similar facilities and who won frequently, became national celebrities on a par with today's greatest boxing, football, and basketball stars. The crowds that applauded and loudly cheered them from the stands were composed of a mix of men and women, rich and poor, and free and slave, for anyone could attend as long as they could find a place to sit or stand. The circus was also a social center where people visited with friends, negotiated business deals, or flirted with prospective lovers between races, as well as consumed all manner of foods sold in snack bars located beneath the stands. There were also gamblers, loan sharks, prostitutes, and pickpockets roaming the facility. As one modern scholar memorably put it, the Great Circus was "literally a meeting place for the Roman world."

Formal, large-scale public games such as chariot races and gladiatorial fights were not the only games the Romans enjoyed. They also engaged in numerous informal, smaller-scale sports and sportslike activities. These included ball playing, swimming, boating, hunting, fishing, mountain climbing, and several others. Of these, they were especially fond of ball games of many different varieties. Such games took place in gyms, bathhouses, private clubs, and most often the streets.

Unfortunately, evidence concerning the rules and specific moves of most ancient ball games is scarce. And scholars still argue over which were team sports, which were individual contests, and exactly how they were played. One popular ball game was evidently similar to but a good deal rougher than "keep away," commonly played in modern grade schools and junior high schools. The widely respected second-century A.D. Greek doctor Galen described the game, advocating it as a way to stay in shape.

Galen also praised the game for being "free from risk," when compared to more violent sports like boxing, horse racing, and chariot racing. Perhaps if Scorpus had devoted himself to ball playing instead of the circus he might have lived to a ripe old age. But in that case he would not have achieved everlasting glory, as expressed in an epitaph supplied by his devoted fan Martial: "Here I lie, Scorpus . . . the darling of Rome, wildly cheered, but shortlived."

The Romans' Love of Circuses and Chariot Races

Robert B. Kebric

The Romans had an enormous appetite for formal, large-scale public games, including the famous fights to the death between gladiators and wild animal shows in which humans fought beasts and beasts fought beasts. The most popular of the large-scale games, however, were the chariot races, held in huge oval racetracks called circuses. In this well-informed overview, noted scholar Robert B. Kebric, of the University of Louisville, describes the racing facilities, including the mighty Circus Maximus, in Rome, as well as the drivers, stables, fans, and of course the actual races.

For a thousand years and more, through the administrations of countless magistrates and almost a hundred emperors . . . despite change, upheaval, and transformation, one thing remained constant for the Roman people throughout the generations: their love of circuses and the chariot races that took place in them. . . .

The Circus Maximus

Circuses in Rome were not, as in recent times, assortments of clowns, trapeze artists, acrobats, trained animals, and other specialty acts collected under a "Big Top" and directed by a "Ringmaster.". . . Originally, circuses were multipurpose facilities that functioned foremost as chariot racetracks—mostly for two- and four-horse teams—and as Pliny the Younger contemptuously observed, the races were popular to the extreme:

> I have been spending all the last few days amongst my notes and papers in most welcome peace. How could I—in the city? The

Races were on, a type of spectacle which has never had the slightest attraction for me. I can find nothing new or different in them: once seen is enough, so it surprises me all the more that so many thousands of adult men should have such a childish passion for watching galloping horses and drivers standing in chariots, over and over again. . . . When I think how this futile, tedious, monotonous business can keep them sitting endlessly in their seats, I take pleasure in the fact that their pleasure is not mine. And I have been very glad to fill my idle hours with literary work during these days which others have wasted in the idlest of occupations.

(*Letters* 9.6)

Pliny's disdain for the mindless masses who frequented the races was apparently more the result of snobbery than any real conviction. His true feelings are more accurately gauged by the fact that his own signet ring had a chariot team represented on it! Even Pliny, despite his protestations, had succumbed to the lure of the Circus. . . .

There were dozens of circuses throughout the Empire, and the city of Rome had four major tracks: the Circus Flaminius, laid out in 221 B.C.; the Circus of Caligula and Nero, built in the first century A.D.; the Circus of Maxentius from the early fourth century A.D.; and the oldest and grandest of them all (probably the largest spectator facility ever built), the Circus Maximus. Located in a depression between the Aventine and Palatine Hills, the Circus Maximus sat directly below the Imperial Palace. Its history traditionally went back to the time of the kings—but it did not approach the monumental proportions that would characterize it during the Empire until Julius Caesar established its canonical shape of two long sides ending in a semicircle. Augustus completed Caesar's work, and succeeding emperors continued to improve and rebuild the structure. By 103 A.D., it had reached its most impressive stage with Trajan's massive reconstruction.

The Circus was immense by any standard. Externally, its length was about 680 yards (over a third of a mile), while its width was 150 yards. The most recent estimates place its seating capacity at about 150,000, although some ancient sources make it 250,000 and more. It is difficult to reconcile this discrepancy. Modern figures are based on the best available physical evidence, but the Romans were notorious for overcrowding, and we can never know how many people they actually packed into the Circus. Still, it is not easy to account for an additional 100,000 spectators, and the ancient figures may have included those who watched from the hills overlooking the track. . . .

The arena of the Circus measured about 635 by 85 yards, or roughly twelve times that of the Colosseum, another of Rome's great spectator facilities. Its floor was a bed of compacted earth covered with a layer of sand, designed to allow the chariots to hold the track (especially on the turns), to save the horses from injury, and to drain off water. Attendants carefully maintained the surface before, during, and after a race, and probably wetted it down between contests to limit the dust.

At one end of the Circus were twelve starting gates (*carceres*). Running down the middle of the arena, closer to the rounded end of the facility, was a long, narrow barrier (frequently identified as the *spina* but more accurately called the *euripus*). Approximately 365 yards in length, it was covered with an assortment of shrines, altars, and other monuments, including two large obelisks brought from Egypt. It was around this barrier, which had turning posts (*metae*) at each end, that the chariots whirled seven death-defying times (about 3 miles), always to the driver's left. Seven large bronze dolphins at one end of the barrier and seven "eggs" at the other were used to indicate the lap number. . . . As lap counters, however, the dolphins and eggs probably benefited the crowd more than the charioteers, who were totally involved in the race. They must have depended on personal lap counters who were stationed closer to the track. . . .

Immediately before each race, the presiding magistrate drew lots in front of the crowd to determine which driver's team would occupy each starting gate. Lots did not automatically assign a gate but allowed a charioteer to select the one he wanted. The driver who chose first did not necessarily have an advantage over his competition, for depending on the rest of the draw, what seemed a good choice at the beginning may not have turned out that way in the end. Consequently, it was the skill of the driver and his team that determined the outcome. No one could complain that he had not had an equal opportunity to win at the start.

Once closed behind their gates, the charioteers and their teams waited impatiently for the magistrate to drop a white napkin from a stand above them. The signal activated a mechanism that threw open the doors and released them from their stalls. . . .

During the reign of Augustus, this scene was typically repeated twelve times each racing day. Caligula doubled that number, and twenty-four races daily remained fairly standard. . . .

More than a Racetrack

It would be a mistake to view the Circus as nothing more than a glorified horse-racing facility. Astrologers considered it a microcosm not only of the Roman world but also of the universe, and they based predictions on its configurations and the races. The twelve starting gates, for example, represented the twelve signs of the zodiac; the seven laps, the days of the week; the twenty-four races, the hours of the day; and the turning posts—around which four-horse (the sun) and two-horse (the moon) chariots raced, as heavenly bodies race around the heavens—were representations of East and West.

In the stands, merchants, tradesmen, farmers, soldiers, cooks, bureaucrats, the unemployed, and even slaves shared the same sun with senators, the royal family, and often the emperor himself. Only the Circus's restricted seating prevented social distinctions from dissolving altogether in a moment of frenzy when all cheered their favorites, more demigods than men.

Inside its four-story facade, the Circus was a maze of shops, rooms, stairways, and arcades. Throngs of people moved about the great interior corridor that provided access to any part of the structure. Vendors hawked their wares and sold refreshments and souvenirs; and, of course, there were always prostitutes, gamblers, pickpockets, girl watchers, and drunks.

Since there was some time between races and the races themselves did not last long (certainly less than ten minutes), many spectators probably came outside to watch only for the start of a contest. They stood on the stairs or any place they could find while the race was on, and when it was over, they went back inside. It is doubtful that anyone remained seated during a race, and thousands of transient spectators would have swelled the grandstands considerably past the 150,000 seating capacity during a race.

The Circus, then, was literally a meeting place for the Roman world. During the Empire, it was also the one place where the emperor could communicate with a large segment of the population. It was difficult for the emperor to gauge the needs and sentiments of the people he ruled. In an authoritarian regime, it was almost impossible for the populace to express itself about taxes, high prices, injustices, war, and peace. Both sides could make their feelings known at the Circus. . . .

There were always intermittent protest and riot in the Circus, but . . . it is difficult to accept wholesale the usual characterization of the racing crowd as an undisciplined rabble, always on the verge of eruption. [The first-century A.D. satirist] Juvenal's oft-quoted remark that the population of his day was only interested in "bread and circus games" is an obvious overstatement, made by a man who knew better but was overly concerned with the social ills and morality of his day. The same probably holds true for the historian Tacitus' observation that plebeians had nothing better to do than to hang around places like the Circus. The behavior of the typical Roman fan who attended the Circus was, within the standards of the day, probably no better or worse than that of his or her modern counterpart.

The image of the hapless emperor under constant siege by restless mobs who used the Circus and other spectator facilities as spawning grounds for dissent is unrealistic for most of Roman

Thousands of Romans attended chariot races, the most popular of public games. The immense Circus Maximus was a renowned racing facility.

history. "Riots" took place within recognized boundaries of be-havior. The ruler was to provide for his people and, as long as he did, he received their enthusiastic support. If he did not, the people reacted. Both sides knew how far they could go. . . .

[Emperors] needed to give their subjects diversions that would distract them from daily problems and divert their attention away from politics. Political dissent during the Empire was chan-neled from the polling place to the racing window. Without pub-lic entertainment, general restlessness could ensue, causing pos-sible destabilization of the state and other problems—all more serious than any disturbances that might arise in the stands of the Circus. . . .

As an additional crowd-pleasing tactic, emperors often offered prizes, money, and other treats, including a banquet at the end of the day, to help soothe any aggressions built up over a particularly devastating racing day. It was also good public relations for the emperor to make a personal appearance at the Circus, albeit in his imperial box (*pulvinar*), to make the people feel that he shared their simple pleasures. Emperors who overindulged in the racing scene, however, learned that they had to restrain their enthusi-asm, since their favoritism toward a certain driver or horse could cause fans with similar dispositions to become overconfident and more inclined to violence. Even if an emperor did not care for the races, it was still wise to put in an occasional appearance. . . .

Drivers, Fans, and Factions

While the Circus was many things to many people, the central interest was, of course, the charioteers and their teams. The lat-ter were carefully bred; the former usually lacked any kind of re-spectable pedigree. Most drivers started as slaves or low in the social order, a fact that probably enhanced their image, since they seemed to be free from conventional moral and social restraints. Those from similar backgrounds could identify with their heroes and hope to emulate their success. The status that accrued to these "sand-splattered daredevils" was not unlike—yet still sur-passes—that given to modern-day sports superstars.

Prominent charioteers were chums of some emperors; gilded busts and portraits of the most famous were set up all over town; they were consulted as magicians, since their winning ways could be explained only in terms of magical power. Their wealth was proverbial. Juvenal laments that a driver could net a hundred times the wages of a lawyer (*Satire* 7.112–114), and the poet Martial speaks of fifteen bags of gold won in an hour (10.74). Charioteers' criminal antics—which included "doping" and poisoning rivals' horses (and sometimes the rivals themselves) and "doctoring" races—often spilled over into the public. Nero, himself a professional rowdy and avid fan of the races, was prompted to crack down on charioteers because they molested, robbed, or beat up passersby in the streets. Generally, charioteers were "above the law." The outlandish emperor Elagabalus offered his solution to the problem by making a charioteer his police chief! By the Late Empire, the Prefect of Rome was actually forbidden to punish them.

The reason authorities were so cautious in dealing with charioteers is obvious. Their fans were fanatics and, as with many modern sports enthusiasts, were easily aroused. One loyal supporter supposedly threw himself on the funeral pyre of his deceased hero, while others went so far as to decorate their tombs with images of chariots and the Circus. . . . Even horse dung was in high demand among enthusiasts, who ran about dissecting recent droppings to determine the diet and health of their favorites and rivals.

Each charioteer drove for one of four circus factions (*factiones*), identified by the colors green, blue, red, and white. . . . Fans were devoted more to the faction color than they were to individual drivers, although everyone had their favorite to cheer. When a driver changed factions, he did not take his fans with him, no more than would a modern player if he moved from a team in New York to one in Chicago.

Factions began as little more than professional stables run for profit by private individuals. Magistrates responsible for conducting the races would contract with them to provide horses, drivers, equipment, and other personnel and paraphernalia necessary to stage a competition. Each stable had fans, or partisans, who supported its drivers at the races. Initially, everything needed for a successful day of racing had to be assembled from the ground up each time a meet was held. This was expensive and confusing, and there was little consistency in quality. The rise of professional stables gradually helped to ensure quality and held costs down. However, the popularity of the circuses continued to grow, as did the demand for more races. Costs began to escalate—for which faction heads . . . holding a virtual track monopoly, were mostly responsible. By the Late Empire, the emperors had assumed control over the faction stables, not only because of the financial drain but also because of the increasing political influence and power of the factions. . . .

Races were always between factions—three teams from each if all twelve stalls were filled. Should a foul be committed against one color by another or if a favored driver suffered some humiliation in or outside the Circus, fan reaction could be immediate and violent. Besides emotion, money was involved.

By the fourth century A.D., political instability and declining police supervision led to a dramatic rise in violent circus-related incidents. Riots broke out in Rome in 355 A.D. when the charioteer Filoromus was arrested. In 390 A.D., seven thousand people were massacred at Thessalonica in Greece, reputedly as a result of rioting over the arrest of a favorite for making homosexual advances toward a general. The general was lynched by the mob! Charioteers became ringleaders for so many kinds of public disturbances that in 394 A.D. the Emperor Theodosius banned the display of their pictures everywhere except at the entrance to circuses. . . .

Christian writers had already become convinced that the circuses were the Devil's playground. Tertullian warned members of his flock to stay clear of them or risk endangering their immortal souls. Even faced with such a prospect, Christians did not let their seats in the Circus get cold, for the races continued well into the Christian era, the last recorded contest at Rome occurring in 549 A.D.

The Career of Diocles

Of the great charioteers adored by Roman crowds and made immortal by their antics, few rivaled Gaius Appuleius Diocles . . . from Spain. His career is the best documented of any driver we know. During the reigns of Hadrian and Antoninus Pius, Diocles completed a twenty-four-year career that brought him fabulous wealth, prestige, and recognition throughout the Empire. Only a handful of charioteers over the centuries could boast of similar achievements. In his day, Diocles practically owned the Circus Maximus.

Diocles competed in 4,257 races and was victorious on 1,462 occasions. . . .

He began his career with the Whites in 122 A.D. when he was eighteen, and it was two long years before his first victory. In 128 A.D., he transferred to the Greens, but he had joined the Reds by 131 A.D. This was a bold move because of the popularity of the Greens, but Diocles suffered no apparent damage. He racked up hundreds of victories for the Reds before his retirement fifteen years later at age forty-two. . . .

Diocles' races were almost exclusively in the four-horse chariot, or *quadrigae,* and, in addition to his numerous triumphs, he also placed 1,438 times (most of them seconds). Even the best, however, sometimes come up empty, and Diocles failed to place in 1,351 races. He was no less a "superstar," for 1,064 of his victories came in single-entry races that pitted the best driver from each stable against one another. The prestige of winning such races is clear. Diocles' admirers, comparing his victories with those of a Blue driver named Epaphroditus, pointed out that while the latter had more wins, only 911 were in the single-entry races—153 short of Diocles' impressive total!

Diocles also captured 110 crowns in opening races, which attracted great attention. These races followed a splendid street parade, and the charioteers participating in the races were part of the procession. Consequently, this initial contest was something like a "feature race" with special significance attached to it.

In almost a third of his victories, Diocles won in the final stretch. More often than not, he held the lead from start to finish. In team-entry races that pitted two or even three chariots (we know of only one case of four) from one stable against the same number from the other stables, Diocles won 398 victories. In these races, success depended less on individual skill than it did on team effort. The stable's "number one" driver was assisted by secondary drivers, whose main function was to interfere with the opposition and help him win. . . .

Diocles may not have been any better than some of Rome's other celebrated charioteers, but he did have one advantage over most of them: He lived to enjoy his wealth and fame. The racetrack was a frequent scene of tragedy, and many drivers met their deaths there. A driver could be crushed against the barrier or lose a wheel; wrapping the ends of the long horse reins around his waist could be fatal if he could not reach the knife in his belt to cut himself free in an emergency; fouling and interfering with his opponents during a race could have dangerous consequences, as could risky displays of showmanship. A brief life was often abruptly ended on a sunny Roman afternoon, and the premature demise of a luminary such as [the popular driver] Scorpus brought the pens of even Rome's greatest poets to life. Martial sorrowfully noted the latter's passing at the end of the first century A.D. and spoke of him in the most glowing terms:

> Let grieving Victory tear to pieces her Idumaean palms, and you, Adoration, beat your naked breast with cruel hands. Let Honor put on mourning, and sad Glory cut her hair once crowned with victory, and throw it as an offering on the wanton flames of the pyre. Alas, foul trick of Fortune! Cheated of the flower of your youth, Scorpus, you are fallen, and all too soon you harness the dark horses of Death. Why did the finishing post to which you did so often hasten with speedy course in your chariot become the finish of your own life?
>
> (*Epigrams* 10.50)

Martial also composed an epitaph for Scorpus:

> I am Scorpus, the glory of the roaring Circus, the object of Rome's cheers, and her short-lived darling. The Fates, counting not my years but the number of my victories, judged me to be an old man.
>
> (*Epigrams* 10.53)

Eyewitness to Victory in the Great Circus

Sidonius Apollinaris

The fifth-century A.D. Roman poet Sidonius Apollinaris composed this exciting account (translated by Jo-Ann Shelton) of a chariot race that took place in the famous Circus Maximus, or "Great Circus," in Rome. Sidonius's friend, the charioteer Consentius, was the victor. For his prize, he received a palm branch, a common symbol of victory. Substantial purses were also awarded in many races, but most of this money went to the owner of the winning horses and chariot. (Sometimes the owner shared some of the purse with the charioteer, especially if the latter was famous and popular.)

[The four chariot teams enter the starting gates.] The four team colors are clearly visible: white and blue, green and red. [The drivers wore tunics dyed in these colors. Each color represented a distinct racing organization, or faction, a private stable owned by a businessman, a *dominus factionis*.] Grooms are holding the heads and the bridles of the horses, . . . calming them with soothing pats and reassuring them with words of encouragement. Still the horses fret in the gates, lean against the starting barrier, and snort loudly. . . . They rear up, prance, and kick impatiently against the wood of the gates. A shrill blast of the trumpet, and the chariots leap out of the gates, onto the track. . . . The wheels fly over the ground, and the air is choked with the dust stirred up on the track. The drivers urge their horses with whips. Standing in the chariots, they lean far forward so that they can whip even the shoulders of the horses. . . . The chariots fly out of sight, quickly covering the long open stretch. . . . When they have come around the far turn, both the rival teams have passed Consentius, but his partner is in the lead. The middle teams concentrate now on taking the lead in the in-

Sidonius Apollinaris, "Poems," *As the Romans Did: A Source Book in Roman Social History*, edited and translated by Jo-Ann Shelton. New York: Oxford University Press, 1988. Copyright © 1988 by Oxford University Press, Inc. Reproduced by permission.

side lane. [The drivers vied for the inside lane because the distance of a lap in this position was somewhat shorter than in the outer lanes.] If the driver in front pulls his horses too far right toward the spectator stands, he leaves an opening on his left, in the inside lane. [The chariots raced counterclockwise, so that all the turns were to the left. They were also quite sharp—close to 180 degrees, making them very difficult to maneuver without veering off sideways and losing precious time.]

The Cheers of the Spectators

Consentius, however, redoubles his efforts to hold back his horses and skillfully reserve their energy for the seventh and last lap. The others race full out, urging their horses with whip and voice. The track is moist with the sweat of both horses and drivers. . . . And thus they race, the first lap, the second, the third, the fourth. In the fifth lap, the leader is no longer able to withstand the pressure of his pursuers. He knows his horses are exhausted, that they can no longer respond to his demand for

A Charioteer Boasts of His Victories

Those charioteers that became widely popular with racing fans received a portion of the victory purse, so a few drivers became quite wealthy. One such successful charioteer—Gaius Appuleius Diocles, proudly ordered this list of his victories to be set down in an inscription, which has survived.

Gaius Appuleius Diocles, driver for the Red Faction.
    Born in Lusitania, Spain. 42 years, 7 months, 23 days old.
    He drove first for the White faction, beginning in A.D. 122, and won his first victory, in A.D. 124, for the same faction. In A.D. 128, he drove for the first time with the Green faction. In A.D. 131, he won his first victory for the Red faction.
    Statistics: He drove four-horse chariots for 24 years. He had 4257 starts, 1462 first-place finishes, 110 of them in opening races. [The opening race was viewed as the most important of the day.] In single-entry races [those that feature four drivers, one from each faction] he had 1064 first-place finishes, winning 92 major purses, 32 of them worth 30,000 sesterces (three of these finishes were with six-horse teams), 28 of them worth 40,000 sesterces (two with six-horse teams), 29 worth 50,000 sesterces (one with a seven-horse team), and 3 worth 60,000 sesterces.

speed, and he pulls them aside. When the sixth lap had been completed and the crowd was already demanding that the prize be awarded, Consentius's opponents thought they had a very safe lead for the seventh and last lap, and they drove with self-confidence, not a bit worried about a move by Consentius. But suddenly he loosens the reins, plants his feet firmly on the floorboard, leans far over the chariot, . . . and makes his fast horses gallop full out. One of the other drivers tries to make a very sharp turn at the far post, feeling Consentius close on his heels, but he is unable to turn his four wildly excited horses, and they plunge out of control. Consentius passes him carefully. The fourth driver is enthralled by the cheers of the spectators and turns his galloping horses too far right toward the stands. Consentius drives straight and fast, and passes the driver who has angled out and only now, too late, begun to urge his horses with the whip. The latter pursues Consentius recklessly, hoping to overtake him. He cuts in sharply across the track. His horses lose their balance and fall. Their legs become tangled in the spinning

---

In double-entry races [with eight chariots, two from each faction] he had 347 first-place finishes, including 4 with three-horse teams and purses of 15,000 sesterces.

In triple-entry races [with twelve drivers, three from each faction] he had 51 wins.

All total, he was in the money 2900 times. Besides his 1462 wins, he was second 861 times, third 576 times, and fourth once, when the fourth prize was 1000 sesterces. He failed to place 1351 times. . . . He won a grand total of 35,863,120 sesterces. [This total went to the faction owner and Diocles received a cut.]

In races for two-horse chariots, he had 3 first-place finishes, 1 tie with the Whites, and 2 with the Greens.

In 815 races, he took the lead at the start and held it to the end.

In 67 races, he came from behind to win. . . .

He won 42 races in various different ways.

He won in the final stretch 502 times, 216 times over the Greens, 205 times over the Blues, and 81 times over the Whites.

He made nine horses hundred-race winners, and one horse a two-hundred-race winner.

Quoted in Jo-Ann Shelton, ed. and trans., *As the Romans Did: A Source Book in Roman Social History.* New York: Oxford University Press, 1988, p. 356.

chariot wheels and are snapped and broken. The driver is hurled headlong out of the shattered chariot which then falls on top of him in a heap of twisted wreckage. His broken and bloody body is still. [Sometimes other chariots crashed into the first to go down, a disaster known as a "shipwreck."] . . . And now the emperor presents the palm branch of victory to Consentius.

Exercise and Small-Scale Sports and Games

J.P.V.D. Balsdon

This tract is from the highly acclaimed book about Roman leisure activities by the late, great classical scholar J.P.V.D. Balsdon. The focus is on small-scale, mostly informal athletics, sports, and activities involving physical exercise, including hunting, Greek-style athletics (wrestling, discus throwing, and so on), swimming, weightlifting, and various ball games. To support his discussion, Balsdon either quotes or mentions several Greek and Roman writers who wrote about such activities. Among them are the great orator Cicero, the poet Horace, and the architect Vitruvius, all Romans of the first century B.C.; the satirists Juvenal and Martial and noted letter-writer Pliny the Younger, all Romans of the first century A.D.; and two second-century A.D. Greeks—the physician Galen and social commentator Athenaeus.

The majority of those who took exercise took it in the afternoon during the eighth and ninth hours—that is, between 1.15 and 3.45 P.M. at midsummer and between 12.45 and 2.15 at midwinter. Young men of the upper social classes in Rome and in the youth organizations *(Iuventus)* were not so restricted in time and must have spent much of their mornings too in arduous physical exercise. These youth organizations for free-born boys of the upper social class, started by Augustus and encouraged by succeeding emperors, spread quickly through the country towns of Italy and, in the first and second centuries A.D., into the western provinces and into Greece. They developed in due course into *'collegia'* with magistrates, and were eventually to perform something of the function of a local militia. They are a part of Roman life which has been brought to light in the main by inscriptions and in particular by the excavations at Pompeii.

J.P.V.D. Balsdon, *Life and Leisure in Ancient Rome.* New York: McGraw-Hill, 1969.

Manly vs. Greek

An aristocracy like the Roman is in its origins an aristocracy of country-dwellers; its sons are brought up to ride and to hunt. Hunting was internationally the sport of aristocrats and of kings. . . . The young aristocrat hunted and, since he must be ready for war if war came, he was trained in the art of fighting. As in medieval times there was jousting; so the young Roman . . . trained with shield and javelin. . . .

When [the Roman poet] Ovid pictured Romulus and Remus [the founders of Rome] exercising themselves in boxing, throwing the javelin and putting the weight, his imagination got the better of his historical sense, for these, like running and wrestling, were sports which reached Rome later, through contact with the Etruscans and the Greek cities in the south. They then became a part of Roman education, starting in boyhood and continuing after the age of fourteen (in *adulescentia*) until the age of seventeen, when military service started. This, Cicero says, was a period of life devoted to exercise and sport in the Campus.

The Campus in Republican Rome was the Campus Martius, described by [the Greek traveler] Strabo as 'a vast area with unlimited space for driving chariots and riding and at the same time for all the people playing ball, trundling hoops and wrestling.' Those exercising were mainly youths, but older men were to be seen—prodigious sights sometimes, like [the military general] Marius when he was nearly seventy, 'practising weapon drill and riding every day among the young people', and the younger Cato, 'oiling himself and playing ball' after his failure to secure election to the consulship in 52 B.C. The runners were oiled, the wrestlers oiled and dusted. At the end of their exercise they plunged into the neighbouring Tiber. 'So the Romans of old, who from successive wars and incessant danger acquired mastery of the art of war, selected the Campus Martius as being near the Tiber so that, after their fighting exercises were finished, the young people might wash off the sweat and dust and by hard swimming recover from the exhaustion of the races.' They still swam in the Tiber after their sports in Cicero's time and later.

Relaxation of this hard military training was no doubt considered by some to be a part of the decadence which attacked the wealthy aristocracy especially in the years after Sulla's dictator-

ship [in the 80s B.C.]. Horace once complained bitterly that contemporary Roman boys had not been taught to ride and were
frightened of hunting; they would rather indulge in Greek
sport—just as English traditionalists complained in the late nine-
teenth century when hunting and rowing, both manly sports,
were challenged by the new organized games which appealed so
strongly to the public schools and the middle classes. Hunting the
hare and breaking in a horse were for Horace '*Romana militia*', in
contrast to other exercises, whose devotees were 'playing the
Greek'. Cicero, however, considered exercise and sport in the
Campus on a par with hunting as unexceptionable relaxation.

By the late Republic and early Empire there were three sorts
of exercise or sport. In the oldest and best tradition of the Roman
aristocracy were hunting, riding and competition in arms. (No
mention is made of horse jumping.) Second came the sports
which ranked highest in Greek esteem: boxing, wrestling, running, throwing the discus and the javelin. There were also swimming and jumping, both part of the recruit's training in the army.
Lastly there were weight-lifting, trundling a hoop and a great variety of ball games. Rowing was never a serious Roman sport.

Boxing and wrestling were sports of emperors. Augustus was
an enthusiastic spectator of boxing. Marcus Aurelius enjoyed
boxing and wrestling; a man should face life, he thought, as a
wrestler, prepared for any contingency. He also hunted and
played ball. The young Gratian in the fourth century . . . ran fast,
wrestled skilfully, high-jumped well, threw the javelin and cast
darts with great skill and was also an excellent horseman.

Student Athletics

Julius Caesar had been an excellent rider and was skilled in
weapon-fighting, and [his great-nephew and the future emperor
Augustus] Octavian, though he did not match his great-uncle's
skill, kept up his riding and his arms-drill until the civil wars were
over. He then decided that the training of boys and youths in military exercises and sport was to be an important feature of Roman life, and [after gaining the title of Augustus] inaugurated
the Youth Movement, the *Iuventus*. In Rome he revived the *Lusus
Troiae*, an immensely complicated military [exercise] . . . not unlike a medieval tournament, in which the young sons of the aris-

tocracy, after ceremonial riding and counter-riding, engaged in mock battle, and then re-formed. . . .

The *tirones* of the new youth organizations were boys at school, taking—in the manner of English public school boys—a great deal of exercise; and it is no accident that on the stucco reliefs of the ceiling of the central nave of the underground basilica of the Porta Maggiore at Rome, the scene in which a seated schoolmaster is watching a pupil in some part of his schooling is directly above another in which three boys are playing ball and two others, exercising with shields and short swords or staves, are being supervised by a coach. On the opposite side of the same ceiling two boys with shields and light swords are attacking wooden posts, *pali* (as recruits did both in the army and in gladiatorial schools), again under the supervision of instructor. . . .

Members of the *Iuventus* not only paraded ceremonially in public; they also played games and competed in sport before spectators. If they fought sometimes in the manner of gladiators, as [the emperor] Vespasian's son Titus once did in his home town, it was with this difference, that they were amateurs, while gladiators were professionals, and they fought with dummy weapons, not to kill. Medieval tournaments were . . . 'military exercises carried out not in the spirit of hostility but solely for practice and display of prowess', and young Romans trained and demonstrated the results of their training in similar displays. *Graffiti* from the great Palaestra in Pompeii show that, just as 'jousters travelled from land to land . . . offering and accepting challenges' teams of *iuvenes* from one town engaged in competitions with teams from another.

Ball Games

For most grown men, particularly in the baths, exercise took the form of one or other of different games of ball. Manuals of instruction were published, which do not survive; but we have Galen's interesting little essay 'On Exercise with the Small Ball,' in which he discussed exercise in general, stressing its psychological side—the greater the enjoyment derived from it, the better—and insisting that, at its best, it should bring every muscle of the body into play. Hunting, the best exercise of all, was expensive and time-consuming; it was therefore barred to men in public life and to those who had their living to earn. The 'small ball game', better than wrestling or running because it exercised every part of the body, took up little time and cost nothing. It was a profitable training in strategy; serious accidents were rare and, as it could be played with varying degrees of strenuousness, it was a good game for men of all ages.

The 'small ball game' *par excellence* was *harpastum,* and was the game which the Greek world had once called *phaininda.* . . . It was certainly played with a hard ball, and 'dusty' was the epithet which Martial used of it. It was perhaps a little more dangerous than Galen suggested, for we know of a spectator who became involved and had his leg broken. Athenaeus wrote of the game as follows:

> The game called *harpastum,* was formerly called *phaininda,* which is the kind I like best of all.

> Great are the exertion and fatigue attendant upon contests of ball playing, and violent twisting and turning of the neck. Hence Antiphanes, 'Damn me, what a pain I've got in my neck.' He describes the game of *phaininda* thus: 'He seized the ball and passed it with a laugh to one, while the other player he dodged; from one he pushed it out of the way, while he raised another player to his feet amid resounding shouts of 'Out of bounds', 'Too far', 'Right beside him', 'Over his head', 'On the ground', 'Up in the air', 'Too short', 'Pass it back in the scrum'.

Scholarship has done its best to reconstruct the rules of the game, but in the absence of any surviving representation of it, whether in painting or in stone relief, little is to be gained by such speculation. We can only be certain that, like the Greek *episkyros,* it was a team game.

Other ball games were individual games, played only by two or three players. Two men might throw and catch a small hand ball. . . . You threw one way to a tall opponent, another way to a short one; you sent a difficult ball to a skilled player, and practically handed the ball to your opponent if he was an unskilled beginner. A player who exhibited *malignitas* [poor sportsmanship] spoiled the game.

If there were three players, they stood as if at the three points of a triangle and the game, called *trigon* (as was the hard ball with which it was played), was a serious matter, each player having his own—often very raucous—scorer and his own ball-boy. . . .

More balls than one might be in play, and each player feinted, trying to mislead his opponents as to the direction in which he was about to throw the ball. . . . A good player was a man of quick reactions and great agility. . . .

The scorer evidently counted missed catches which dropped to the ground; so that the winner was the player with the smallest score. Only if this was the case, can sense be made of Martial's sycophant [toady or yes-man] in the baths who, evidently standing behind the player whom he wanted to flatter, caught in either hand the balls which this player missed. It is surprising that the other two players did not protest—unless they too had similar supporters behind them. For when *trigon* was played at the baths, it was evidently common for others who were exercising . . . to stand round and watch. . . .

There was a third game—'*expulsim ludere*'—in which the ball was thrown against a wall. You might see slaves or children doing this in the street. . . . The player took the ball off the wall full-toss or else at the first bounce. . . . This game, unlike the others, was evidently played in a special court. Such courts (*sphaeristeria*) existed, no doubt, in a great many baths . . . and also in a number of private villas. There was one in the younger Pliny's Laurentine villa and another in his villa in Tuscany. . . . A court was evidently partly open, and was sited so as to receive the afternoon sun, that being the time when exercise was normally taken. . . .

However the ball game which most middle-aged and elderly men played before their bath was less vigorous than any of these. Whether or not in any very strongly competitive spirit, they threw and caught a larger and lighter ball, either a *paganica*, which was stuffed with feathers, or a *follis*, which was inflated with air—a medicine ball, in fact. . . . Martial describes this as a ball for small boys and for old men. Augustus played it when he abandoned serious exercise after the civil wars; Pliny's elderly friend Spurinna played it at the age of seventy-seven. . . .

Female Athletes and Gyms

Ball-players, strenuous or lethargic, apart, there were young men who fenced with staves (*clavae*) [wooden poles] or tilted at posts; there were the weight-lifters and men exercising with dumbbells; and there were others who indulged in one or other of the exercises in which the *Iuventus* was trained—who ran, rode, drove chariots and wrestled. There were men . . . who spent the entire day in taking exercise.

And what of women?

There are occasional representations in art of young women throwing balls, either alone, to one another, or against a wall; but there is nothing anywhere comparable with the early fourth-century mosaic from Piazza Armerina in Sicily, where a number of agile young women, stripped for exercise, are seen, two running (one of them perhaps a trainer), two playing with a light ball, one throwing the discus and one running with dumb-bells in both hands.

It is to be assumed, therefore, that some women took exercise, in particular that they played the gentler ball games—but to a far smaller extent than men; for women's baths, where they have survived, seem not to have had access, like men's, to *palaestrae* [gyms].

Juvenal and Martial were interested only in the abnormalities of the female sex—in the woman who stripped and played *harpastum*, lifted heavy weights, wrestled and submitted to the severe training of the gladiator. 'Think of a poor husband present at the sale of his wife's property, seeing her gladiatorial kit, whether as Thracian or as Samnite, coming under the hammer.' And there were rare occasions, under Nero and the Flavians, when women fought wild beasts or took part in gladiatorial engagements at public spectacles. . . . These were exceptional women—as, one hopes, was Juvenal's hostess, who after heavy exercise and massage, took a sweat bath and a heavy drink to follow, just as if she was a man, and, just like a man, was flushed and violently sick afterwards when welcoming her dinner guests, again to the horror of the poor husband.

Except for chariot driving and riding, for which, as a general rule, greater space must have been needed, exercise took place in the *palaestrae*, which from late Republican times onwards were attached to the baths, in the open when the weather allowed [or] under the surrounding porticoes [roofed porches] when the sun was too fierce or the weather too cold for exercise in the open air. Vitruvius' remark that the building of *palaestrae* was unusual in Italy is at first sight surprising. The Republican Stabian baths of Pompeii, after all, had their *palaestra*. But Vitruvius wrote before 27 B.C., before the inauguration of the new Youth Movement by Augustus. This movement is seen by the archaeologists as the background to the construction of two new and magnificent *palaestrae*, one by the amphitheatre at Pompeii, a vast enclosure surrounded by porticoes, planted with beautiful trees and provided with a swimming bath (*piscina*) and the other, one third smaller, at Herculaneum, not all of which has yet been exposed, which also had a swimming bath. After this, towns of the western Empire increasingly copied what had long been an important amenity in Greek towns of importance in the East.

Rome's Leading Doctor Advocates Vigorous Exercise

Galen

Many Romans performed some kind of sport or other regular physical exercise, partly out of enjoyment, partly from tradition, and to some degree from the advice of doctors like Galen (ca.A.D. 129–99), a Greek who became the foremost medical practitioner in the Roman Empire. He started out as a physician to gladiators in his native town of Pergamum (in Asia Minor). Thanks to his consummate skills, both at healing and medical writing, his reputation steadily grew. Ultimately he became the highly trusted and respected personal physician to the emperor Marcus Aurelius and some of his successors. The following work—*The Exercise with the Small Ball*—was one of several Galen wrote between A.D. 169 and 175. In it, he advocates regular exercise, especially a vigorous kind of ball game that utilizes most or all of the muscles in the body. (The exact object and rules of the game remain unclear, but it appears to have been some sort of combination of dodgeball and keep away.) Galen also touts the psychological benefits of this game, saying that it can make a person feel better, and its moral virtue as well.

Physical exercise . . . is of considerable importance for health. Its predominance over food was established in the past by the best philosophers and doctors; but the great superiority of the exercise with the small ball has not been sufficiently demonstrated by anyone. So it seems right to me to put down what I know on the subject. . . .

In my opinion, the best exercises of all are those which are able not only to exert the body, but also delight the soul. Those who hit upon hunting—hunting with dogs and all other kinds—found a way of combining exertion with pleasure, delight, and love of honour; they were wise men who well understood human nature. The motion of the soul involved is so powerful that many have been released from their disease by the pleasure alone; many have been completely cured. No bodily affection is so great that it can dominate those of the soul. One should do more than just not ignore the question of what the motions of the soul should be; one should take much greater care of them than of the body's, particularly because the soul is so much greater than the body. This is a common feature of all forms of exercise that involve pleasure; but there are others special to the exercise with the small ball which I shall now enumerate [explain].

A Democratic Form of Exercise

First, there is its accessibility. If you consider how much preparation and leisure are necessary for hounds and all other hunting equipment, you will readily understand that no one in public life, or any practitioner of the arts, can possibly take part in such exercise. It requires considerable wealth and a great deal of free time. The form of exercise we are considering, on the other hand, is the only one which is so democratic that anyone, no matter how small his income, can take part. You need no nets, no weapons, no horses, no hounds—just a single ball, and a small one at that.

It is, moreover, well adjusted to other types of physical activity, so that none of these need suffer as a result of it. What practice could be more convenient than one which is suited to every level of human fortune and to every human activity? The ability to engage in the exercise afforded by hunting is something which the individual cannot determine; it requires money for the outlay on the equipment and leisure to enable one to await the right moment for the hunt. The equipment required for our exercise, on the other hand, is accessible to the means of the poorest of persons; and even a very busy man should be able to find the time for it.

So much, then, for accessibility. Our exercise is also the most sufficient of all. This fact can best be apprehended from a consideration of the capacity and nature of each of the other kinds of exercise. It will be seen that they are all either too vigorous or too mild, or that they move, say, the lower part more than the upper, or some part to the exclusion of the rest—such as the loins, head, hands, or chest. The capacity both to move all parts of the body equally, and also to be practised in either an extremely vigorous or an extremely mild form, is something found in no other exercise except that with the small ball. It may be partially fierce and partially slow, or partially violent and partially gentle, in accordance with the individual's wishes and the apparent needs of his body. And it may, as required, move all parts equally, or some more than others.

When, for example, people face each other, vigorously attempting to prevent each other from taking the space between, this exercise is a very heavy, vigorous one, involving much use of the hold by the neck, and many wrestling holds. And so the head and neck are exerted by these holds by the neck, and the lungs, chest, and stomach by the laying hold, pushing away, and levering involved in such clinches, as well as the other wrestling-style holds. The loins and legs are also subject to great strain in this kind of activity; it requires great steadiness on one's feet. Advancing and leaping to the side, too, represent a considerable exercise for the legs; in fact, this is really the only process in which all their parts are moved in the correct way. The act of coming forward exercises one set of nerves and muscles to a greater extent, the act of retreating another; and that of dodging to the side another still. The concentration on one type of motion of the legs, meanwhile, as in running, provides an unbalanced, unequal type of exercise.

A Skilled Guard and Thief

And as with the legs, so with the arms too, the exercise with the small ball is best from all points of view. For in this case too the variety of forms which the exercise takes means that different muscles are extended at different times; thus all are both exerted and rested equally in the course of the activity; and in this alternation between activity and rest no muscle remains idle throughout, nor does any become strained by constant exertion.

The sense of sight is also exercised; this becomes clear when we consider that anyone failing accurately and quickly to perceive the trajectory of the ball must miss his catch. The mental faculties, moreover, are sharpened by the concern not to drop the ball and to prevent the opponent from seizing it. For though such concern or worry in itself leads to thinning, when combined with some exercise which is connected with a pride in success and is able to cause pleasure, it is of the greatest benefit both to the health of the body and the intelligence of the soul.

In fact, this capacity to assist both body and soul towards their respective excellences is one of the great qualities of this form of exercise. It is fairly easy to see that it has the power to give both of them the most important types of training—those which the rulers of a city would especially command their generals to undertake. The task of a good general involves attacking at the right time, seizing one's opportunity, appropriating the enemy's possessions either by force or by unexpected attack, and keeping guard over what has already been acquired. In short, a general should be a skilled guard and thief; these are the absolutely central features of his art. I can think of no other exercise which provides the same degree of practice in guarding what one has already gained, recovering what one has lost, or anticipating the enemy's policy; and I should be very surprised if anyone else can. Most exercises, in fact, have the opposite effect on the intellect, rendering it idle, sleepy, and slow; and indeed the kind of physical exercise practised in the wrestling school promotes rather the quantity of flesh than the cultivation of virtue. Many have been so thickened by it that they suffer from breathing difficulties. The products of such training will hardly have the capacity for brilliant generalship, or for the charge of power or political affairs; one would be better off placing such matters in the charge of a pig.

It might be thought that I would approve of running, or other such exercises which thin the body. But this is not the case. For lack of proportion is in all cases to be deplored. Proportion is the aim to be cultivated in every art; any loss in this respect is a defect. . . . Purely in the context of health, too, such activity fails, to the extent that it provides an unequal exercise of the different parts of the body. In this process some are bound to be overstretched while others remain entirely idle. Neither of these features is beneficial; in fact, both are causes of the germination of the seeds of disease, as well as the production of an enfeebled state of the faculties.

The Game's Gentle Side

The form of exercise most deserving of our attention is therefore that which has the capacity to provide health of the body, harmony of the parts, and virtue in the soul; and all these things are true of the exercise with the small ball. It is able to benefit the soul in every way; and it causes equal exertion in all parts of the body. At the same time it is extremely beneficial for health, and brings about a well-balanced condition, without any undue accumulation of flesh or excess thinness. It is adequate for the purposes of actions requiring strength and also well suited to those which require speed.

Now it is true that the vigour of this exercise is equal to that of any other exercise, in any respect. But let us again consider its extreme gentleness: there are times when this too is required. This may be because the individual is at an age where he is not yet—or no longer—able to undergo heavy labour, and therefore wishes to reduce the exertion, or it may be that he is recovering from illness. In this context too I believe that our exercise is superior to all others: if one engages in it gently, then no other is equally gentle. One must then adopt a middle position, not moving from the median, and alternate between gentle advances and remaining in the same place; and after a fairly short period of exercise undergo soft massage with olive oil and hot baths.

This is the gentlest form of all, and even for those in need of rest it is highly beneficial. It also has a very high capacity for restoring weakened faculties, as well as being extremely useful for old men and children. But other forms of exercise may also be practised with the small ball, which are stronger than these but still gentler than the most vigorous type. These too should be known to anyone who intends to learn the correct practice in its entirety. If, moreover, as frequently happens as a result of the performance of some necessary task, one exerts either the upper or the lower parts disproportionately, or exerts only the hands or feet, this exercise will enable one to rest the parts which were previously exerted while providing a compensatory degree of exertion to those which were previously idle. If, for example, one throws energetically from a considerable distance, one is using the legs little if at all; and thus one rests the lower parts while giving vigorous exercise to the upper. If, on the other hand, one runs more, and throws quickly, from a great distance, but less often, one will exert the lower parts to a greater extent. And that part of the exercise which involves urgency and speed without great intensity exercises the breath more, while the vigorous part of it, that is, what involves holds, throws, and catches, and yet is not swift, tends rather to tone and strengthen the body. If the movements are both intense and urgent, then there will be great exertion of both body and breath; this is the most vigorous of all possible exercises. . . .

Free from Risk

Let us turn towards the conclusion of our argument. I should not like to omit from my account of the positive attributes of this exercise the fact that it is free from risk. This is not true of most other sorts of exercise. Running, for example, has frequently killed people, by the rupture of a vital vessel; and similarly the phenomenon of loud, violent sounds being produced all at once has been known to cause very great harm in a number of cases. Vigorous horse-riding can cause ruptures in the region of the kidneys, as well as damage in the chest area, or even sometimes in the spermatic channels. And we have not even considered the frequent mistakes made by the horse, as a result of which the rider may be thrown and immediately die. The jump, the discus, and the exercise involving turning have also caused many injuries. I need hardly mention the numbers injured in the [boxing] ring, all of whom seem to have suffered a maiming. . . .

They may be observed to be lame, disfigured, crushed, or at least mutilated in some part or other. Since the exercise with the small ball has, in addition to those already listed, the advantage that it does not involve any danger, then surely it must be the most beneficial exercise of all.

Chronology

B.C.

ca. 1000

Latin tribesmen establish small villages on some of the seven hills marking the site of the future city of Rome.

753

Traditional founding date for the city of Rome by Romulus (as computed and accepted by Roman scholars some seven centuries later).

509

The leading Roman landowners throw out their last king and establish the Roman Republic.

ca. 450–451

The Twelve Tables, constituting Rome's first law code, are inscribed and set up.

340–338

Rome defeats the Latin League, an alliance of Italian city-states, and incorporates the territories of some of its members into the growing Roman state.

312

The building of Rome's first major road, the Appian Way, and its first aqueduct, the Aqua Appia, begins.

280–275

The Romans fight several battles with the Greek Hellenistic king Pyrrhus, who has come to the aid of the Greek cities of southern Italy; his victories are so costly that he abandons the Italian Greeks to their fate.

265

Having gained control of the Italian Greek cities, Rome is master of the whole Italian peninsula.

264–241
Years of the First Punic War, in which Rome defeats the maritime empire of Carthage.

218–201
Rome fights Carthage again in the Second Punic War, in which the Carthaginian general Hannibal crosses the Alps, invades Italy, and delivers the Romans one crippling defeat after another.

200–197
The Romans defeat Macedonia in the Second Macedonian War.

149–146
Rome annihilates Carthage in the Third Punic War.

100
Birth of Julius Caesar, one of the greatest statesmen and military generals in history.

ca. 80
The first all-stone Roman amphitheater opens in the town of Pompeii.

73–71
The Thracian slave Spartacus leads the last of Rome's large slave rebellions; the Roman nobleman Marcus Crassus eventually defeats the slaves.

65
Caesar stages the first large public gladiatorial combats in Rome.

58–51
Caesar conquers the peoples of Transalpine Gaul.

49
Caesar crosses the Rubicon River, initiating a civil war; the following year he defeats his chief rival, Pompey, at Pharsalus (in Greece).

44

After declaring himself "dictator for life," Caesar is assassinated by a group of senators.

42

Roman strongmen Mark Antony and Octavian (Caesar's adopted son) defeat the leaders of the conspiracy against Caesar at Philippi (in northern Greece). At this point, the Republic is effectively dead.

31

Octavian defeats Antony and Egypt's Queen Cleopatra at Actium (in western Greece) and gains firm control of the Mediterranean world. Soon, the Senate confers on him the title of Augustus, "the revered one," and he becomes, in effect, Rome's first emperor.

ca. 30 B.C.–A.D. 180

The approximate years of the so-called Pax Romana ("Roman Peace"), a period in which the Mediterranean world under the first several Roman emperors enjoys relative peace and prosperity.

20

Augustus sets up a board of curators to manage Italy's public highways.

4

Jesus is born in Bethlehem (in the Roman province of Judaea).

A.D.

6

Augustus establishes a fire-fighting force (the *vigiles*) to protect the Roman capital.

14

Augustus dies, plunging the Roman people into a period of deep mourning; he is succeeded by Tiberius.

ca. 30–33

Jesus is executed on the orders of Pontius Pilate, the Roman governor of Judaea.

64

A great fire ravages large sections of Rome; the emperor Nero blames the disaster on the Christians and initiates the first of a series of persecutions against them.

79

The volcano Mt. Vesuvius erupts, burying the Italian towns of Pompeii and Herculaneum; the great naturalist Pliny the Elder dies while observing the disaster up close.

80

The emperor Titus inaugurates the Colosseum, Rome's greatest amphitheater.

98–117

Reign of the emperor Trajan, in which the Roman Empire reaches its greatest size and power.

ca. 122

The emperor Hadrian visits Britain and plans the construction of the massive defensive wall that will bear his name.

180

Death of the emperor Marcus Aurelius, marking the end of the Pax Romana era and beginning of Rome's steady slide into economic and political crisis.

212

The emperor Caracalla extends citizenship rights to all free adult males in the Empire.

235–284

The Empire suffers under the strain of terrible political upheaval and civil strife, prompting later historians to call this period "the Anarchy."

284

Diocletian ascends the throne and initiates sweeping political, economic, and social reforms, in effect reconstructing the Empire under a new blueprint. (Modern historians often call this new realm the Later Empire.)

306–337

Reign of the emperor Constantine I, who carries on the reforms begun by Diocletian.

313

Constantine and his eastern colleague, Licinius, issue the so-called Edict of Milan, granting religious toleration to the formerly hated and persecuted Christians.

330

Constantine founds the city of Constantinople, on the Bosporus Strait, making it the capital of the eastern section of the Empire.

337

Constantine dies; he converts to Christianity on his deathbed.

ca. 370

The Huns, a savage nomadic people from central Asia, sweep into eastern Europe, pushing the Goths and other "barbarian" peoples into the northern Roman provinces.

378

The eastern emperor Valens is disastrously defeated by the Visigoths and Ostrogoths at Adrianople (in northern Greece).

391

At the urgings of Christian leaders, especially the bishop Ambrose, the emperor Theodosius I closes the pagan temples, demolishing some and turning others into museums. In less than a century, Christianity has become the Empire's official religion.

ca. 407

As Rome steadily loses control of several of its northern and western provinces, Britain falls under the sway of barbarian tribes.

426

The great Roman Christian thinker and writer Augustine completes his monumental *City of God*.

476

The German-born general Odoacer demands that the emperor, the young Romulus Augustulus, grant him and his men federate status; when the emperor refuses, Odoacer deposes him and no new emperor takes his place. The succession of Roman emperors continues in the eastern part of the realm, which steadily evolves into the Byzantine Empire.

For Further Research

Ancient Sources in Translation

Apuleius, *The Golden Ass,* trans. P.G. Walsh. Oxford, England: Oxford University Press, 1994.

Catullus, complete poems in *The Poems of Catullus,* ed. and trans. Guy Lee. New York: Oxford University Press, 1990.

Galen, assorted works in *Galen: Selected Works,* trans. P.N. Singer. New York: Oxford University Press, 1997.

Naphtali Lewis and Meyer Reinhold, eds., *Roman Civilization, Sourcebook I: The Republic,* and *Roman Civilization, Sourcebook II: The Empire.* New York: Harper and Row, 1966.

Pliny the Younger, *Letters,* published as *The Letters of the Younger Pliny,* trans. Betty Radice. New York: Penguin Books, 1969.

Seneca, *Letters,* excerpted in Moses Hadas, ed. and trans., *The Stoic Philosophy of Seneca.* New York: W.W. Norton, 1958.

Jo-Ann Shelton, ed. and trans., *As the Romans Did: A Source Book in Roman Social History.* New York: Oxford University Press, 1988.

Modern Sources

Architecture, Houses, Engineering, and Roads

Jean-Pierre Adam, *Roman Building: Materials and Techniques.* Trans. Anthony Mathews. Bloomington: Indiana University Press, 1994.

Lionel Casson, *Travel in the Ancient World.* Baltimore: Johns Hopkins University Press, 1994.

Raymond Chevallier, *Roman Roads,* trans. N.H. Field. Berkeley: University of California Press, 1976.

L. Sprague de Camp, *The Ancient Engineers.* New York: Ballantine Books, 1963.

L.A. Hamey and J.A. Hamey, *The Roman Engineers.* Cambridge, England: Cambridge University Press, 1981.

A.T. Hodge, *Roman Aqueducts and Water Supply.* London: Duckworth, 1992.

William L. MacDonald, *The Architecture of the Roman Empire*. New Haven: Yale University Press, 1982.

Alexander G. McKay, *Houses, Villas, and Palaces in the Roman World*. Baltimore: Johns Hopkins University Press, 1998.

Don Nardo, *Roman Roads and Aqueducts*. San Diego: Lucent Books, 2001.

Colin O'Connor, *Roman Bridges*. Cambridge, England: Cambridge University Press, 1993.

Games and Other Leisure Pursuits

Roland Auguet, *Cruelty and Civilization: The Roman Games*. London: Routledge, 1994.

J.P.V.D. Balsdon, *Life and Leisure in Ancient Rome*. New York: McGraw-Hill, 1969.

Richard C. Beacham, *Spectacle Entertainments of Early Imperial Rome*. New Haven: Yale University Press, 1999.

James H. Butler, *The Theater and Drama of Greece and Rome*. San Francisco: Chandler, 1972.

Alan Cameron, *Circus Factions: Blues and Greens at Rome and Byzantium*. London: Clarendon Press, 1976.

Michael Grant, *Gladiators*. New York: Delacorte Press, 1967.

John H. Humphrey, *Roman Circuses: Arenas for Chariot Racing*. Berkeley: University of California Press, 1986.

Don Nardo, *Games of Ancient Rome*. San Diego: Lucent Books, 2000.

————, *Greek and Roman Theater*. San Diego: Lucent Books, 1995.

General Roman History and Culture

John Boardman et al., *The Oxford History of the Roman World*. New York: Oxford University Press, 1991.

Peter Brown, *The World of Late Antiquity, A.D. 150–750*. New York: Harcourt Brace, 1971.

Matthew Bunson, *A Dictionary of the Roman Empire*. Oxford: Oxford University Press, 1991.

Averil Cameron, *The Later Roman Empire: A.D. 284–430*. Cambridge, MA: Harvard University Press, 1993.

Tim Cornell and John Matthews, *Atlas of the Roman World*. New York: Facts On File, 1982.

T.J. Cornell, *The Beginnings of Rome: Italy and Rome from the Bronze Age to the Punic Wars (c. 1000–264 B.C.)*. London: Routledge, 1995.

Michael Crawford, *The Roman Republic*. Cambridge, MA: Harvard University Press, 1993.

J.A. Crook, *Law and Life of Rome*. Ithaca: Cornell University Press, 1984.

Arther Ferrill, *The Fall of the Roman Empire: The Military Explanation*. New York: Thames and Hudson, 1986.

Michael Grant, *History of Rome*. New York: Scribner's, 1978.

———, *The World of Rome*. New York: New American Library, 1960.

A.H.M. Jones, *The Later Roman Empire, 284–602*. 3 vols. Norman: University of Oklahoma Press, 1964, reprinted 1975.

Anthony Kamm, *The Romans: An Introduction*. London: Routledge, 1995.

Robert B. Kebric, *Roman People*. Mountain View, CA: Mayfield, 1997.

Don Nardo, *The Ancient Romans*. San Diego: Lucent Books, 2001.

———, *The Collapse of the Roman Republic*. San Diego: Lucent Books, 1997.

———, *The Greenhaven Encyclopedia of Ancient Rome*. San Diego: Greenhaven Press, 2002.

———, *The History of Weapons and Warfare: Ancient Rome*. San Diego: Lucent Books, 2003.

Chris Scarre, *Chronicle of the Roman Emperors*. New York: Thames and Hudson, 1995.

Chester G. Starr, *Civilization and the Caesars: The Intellectual Revolution in the Roman Empire*. New York: Norton, 1965.

L.P. Wilkinson, *The Roman Experience*. Lanham, MD: University Press of America, 1974.

Religion and Mythology

John Ferguson, *The Religions of the Roman Empire*. London: Thames and Hudson, 1970.

Robin Lane Fox, *Pagans and Christians*. Harmondsworth, England: Viking Penguin, 1986.

Jane F. Gardner, *Roman Myths*. Austin: University of Texas Press and British Museum Press, 1993.

Michael Grant, *The Myths of the Greeks and Romans*. New York: Penguin Books, 1962.

Georg Luck, *Arcana Mundi: Magic and the Occult in the Greek and Roman Worlds*. Baltimore: Johns Hopkins University Press, 1985.

Ramsay MacMullen, *Christianizing the Roman Empire, A.D. 100–400*. New Haven: Yale University Press, 1984.

Don Nardo, ed., *The Rise of Christianity*. San Diego: Greenhaven Press, 1999.

H.J. Rose, *Religion in Greece and Rome*. New York: Harper, 1959.

H.H. Scullard, *Festivals and Ceremonies of the Roman Republic*. London: Thames and Hudson, 1981.

J.M.C. Toynbee, *Death and Burial in the Roman World*. Baltimore: Johns Hopkins University Press, 1996.

Robert L. Wilken, *The Christians as the Romans Saw Them*. New Haven: Yale University Press, 1984.

Social Institutions, Slavery, and Daily Life

Lesley Adkins and Roy A. Adkins, *Handbook to Life in Ancient Rome*. New York: Facts On File, 1994.

Keith R. Bradley, *Discovering the Roman Family: Studies in Roman Social History*. New York: Oxford University Press, 1991.

———, *Slavery and Society at Rome*. New York: Cambridge University Press, 1994.

F.R. Cowell, *Life in Ancient Rome*. New York: G.P. Putnam's Sons, 1961.

Jane F. Gardner, *Women in Roman Law and Society*. Indianapolis: Indiana University Press, 1986.

Peter Garnsey, *Social Status and Legal Privilege in the Roman Empire*. Oxford: Clarendon Press, 1970.

Michael Grant, *A Social History of Greece and Rome*. New York: Charles Scribner's Sons, 1992.

Harold W. Johnston, *The Private Life of the Romans*. New York: Cooper Square, 1973.

Don Nardo, *Life of a Roman Slave*. San Diego: Lucent Books, 1998.

Sarah B. Pomeroy, *Goddesses, Whores, Wives, and Slaves: Women in Classical Antiquity*. New York: Schocken Books, 1995.

Beryl Rawson, ed., *Marriage, Divorce, and Children in Ancient Rome*. Oxford: Oxford University Press, 1991.

K.D. White, *Roman Farming*. London: Thames and Hudson, 1970.

Index

About the Editor

Historian and award-winning writer Don Nardo has written or edited numerous volumes about ancient Roman history and culture including *The Decline and Fall of the Roman Empire*, *The Age of Augustus*, *Life of a Roman Soldier*, *Games of Ancient Rome*, *Roman Roads and Aqueducts*, the *Greenhaven Encyclopedia of Ancient Rome*, and studies of Julius Caesar and Cleopatra. Mr. Nardo and his wife, Christine, live in Massachusetts.

11/1/03 ✓
AWD

2037840

GAYLORD M